We Were Healed

Rebecca M. Brown

PITTSBURGH, PENNSYLVANIA 15222

The contents of this work including, but not limited to, the accuracy of events, people, and places depicted; opinions expressed; permission to use previously published materials included; and any advice given or actions advocated are solely the responsibility of the author, who assumes all liability for said work and indemnifies the publisher against any claims stemming from publication of the work.

Scriptures and quotations are taken from the Holy Bible, Spirit Filled Life Bible and Amplified Bible.

All Rights Reserved
Copyright © 2008 by Rebecca M. Brown
No part of this book may be reproduced or transmitted in any form or by any means, electronic or mechanical, including photocopying, recording, or by any information storage and retrieval system without permission in writing from the author.

ISBN: 978-1-4349-9086-0
Library of Congress Control Number: 2008923187

Printed in the United States of America

First Printing

For information or to order additional books, please write:
RoseDog Books
701 Smithfield Street
Third Floor
Pittsburgh, Pennsylvania 15222
U.S.A.
1-800-834-1803

Or visit our website and online catalogue at www.rosedogbookstore.com

DEDICATION

This Is Written To Give Praise, Honor and Glory to God

This Book Is Dedicated To:
The Father
The Son
And
The Holy Spirit

This work is dedicated first and foremost to our heavenly Father, the Holy Spirit, and the Lord Jesus Christ. May their blessings and Power flow through every word that is written here in. To my Children, my firstborn (Hilton), James 111, Demetrice, Juan, Shemiaka and Matthew. My daughter-n-law, Stacy (Tyrone & Elnora), Jimmy & Nessie, Nell. To all of my spiritual children. To my grand children, family, and friends. May this work bring much joy and healing to your lives, as the blessing of God continue to flow to and through your lives. May the peace of God stand guard over your hearts and minds, in Jesus Name, Amen!

ACKNOWLEDGMENT

A very special acknowledgment to my loving husband James (Jagg), who has patiently endured my pursuit of God's presence, my call into the ministry and the completion of this work. Thank you for your love and support.

GOD'S CALL

After Many years of wrestling in prayer, studying God's word, seeking God's will, hearing God speak to me, by His spirit and through His word, telling me to go and teach His word, in January of 1992 God stood by my bed one morning at 4 AM and told me, "go now and get you a license, because there are many places I must take you that man will require you to have a license". March 8, 1992; I was licensed to (Teach God's Word).

The Lord continued to visit me, taking me into His word, telling me to study the life of the Prophets, (Jeremiah, Isaiah, Elijah) as I continued to seek God and His will for my life, the Lord commissioned me, He said, "Go, take my word and set the captives free, I've called you as a prophet to the nations, I will use you in my word like a sharp shooter with an eagle's eye, my word will not miss its target. I will send you to the nations of the world. I've put my Spirit in your belly, I've put my word in your mouth, you will teach the uncut version of the word, you will teach the truth. You will lay hands on the sick and they shall be healed from all manner of diseases!"

Jesus Christ, our Lord, the anointed one, has visited me in many dreams and visions. He has spoken many things to me concerning the healing of the sick, and His plans of health, wholeness, peace and prosperity for the saints.

INTRODUCTION

In the twentieth century, sickness and disease have attacked American society on every level, including the Church. Many saints are still struggling with sickness, disease and pain, bearing the effects of the curse of the law. Calvary's double cure is Salvation and healing through the spotless blood of Jesus Christ, the only begotten Son of God, Isaiah saw this and spoke of it hundreds of years before Jesus was born. "Surely He hath borne our griefs, and carried our sorrows: yet we esteem him stricken, smitten of God, and afflicted. But He was wounded for our transgressions, He was bruised for our iniquities; the chastisement of our peace was upon Him; and with His stripes we are healed." (Isaiah 53:4-5)

Peter quotes the frequently used passage from Isaiah, but moves it from future to past tense, indicating that healing has already taken place, <u>it's already done</u>! And it's available to everyone who will believe and receive. "Who his own self bare our sins in His own body on the tree, that we, being dead to sins, should live unto righteousness; by whose stripes we were healed," (1 Peter 2:24)

Christ has redeemed us from the curse of the law, and anything associated with the curse. (Galatians 3:13). The truth is, "By the stripes of Jesus, "We Were Healed." Only by accepting Jesus Christ, the Son of God, as our Healer, and by knowing truth given in the Word of God, can we confront and dispel the strong presence of sickness and disease from the body of Christ and experience healing on the level God intended.

Those who take seriously and act upon the truths presented in this book will obtain a broader understanding about divine healing, their faith will be strengthened, and they will receive the courage to fight for their God given rights to be well and whole.

Many who have attended our Healing Explosions, but failed to receive healing, have later been miraculously healed while listening to the recorded version of the same message that was preached.

He sent His word and healed them. (PS: 107:20)
The Spirit of the Lord is upon me. (St Luke 4:18)
The gospel is power of God unto those who believe. (Romans 1:16)
Lord, who hath believed our report? (Romans 10:16)

When believed and acted upon, the promises of God, the power of God is made available to us. Every promise of God contains the power of God necessary to produce everything it promises. All increase of life within His love comes by His Word. As human response gives place for His blessing. When received, God's word of promise will never be barren or fruitless. The power in His Word will always fulfill the promise of His Word. God's promises are life to those that find them, and health to all their flesh. (Proverbs 4:22).

When these facts became real to me, I decided to put into print this message and offer it to the millions of sufferers to whom I may never minister. I do not pretend to be a writer, nor is any literary style pretended here. My only aim is to make the simplest possible statements which may give my readers a jumpstart to real living, <u>mountain moving faith</u>, and that they will go on to experience such abundance in their lives that they will begin to walk in complete wellness and wholeness in every area of their lives. I just want you to get it!!

> **Who Himself bore our sins in His own body on the tree, that we having died to sins, might live for righteousness...by whose stripes we were healed. (1 Peter 2:24) KJV**
>
> **He personally bore our sins in His [own] body on the tree "[as on an alter and offered Himself on it], that we might die (cease to exist) to sin and live to righteousness. By His wounds you have been healed, (1Peter 2:24) AMP**
>
> **He is despised and rejected by men, A man of sorrows and acquainted with grief. And we hid, as it were, our faces from Him; He was despised, and we did not esteem Him.**
>
> **Surely He has borne our griefs and carried our sorrows, yet we esteemed Him stricken, smitten by God, and afflicted. But he was wounded for our transgressions, He was bruised for our iniquities; The chastisement for our peace was upon Him. And by His stripes we are healed. (Isaiah 53:3-5) KJV**
>
> **He was despised and rejected and forsaken by men, a man of sorrows and pain, and acquainted with**

grief and sickness; and like one from whom men hide their faces, He was despised and we did not appreciate His worth or have any esteem for Him. Surely He has borne our griefs (sicknesses; weaknesses, and distresses) and carried our sorrows and pains [of punishment]. Yet we [ignorantly] considered Him stricken, smitten, and afflicted by God [as if with leprosy]. But He was wounded for our transgressions. He was bruised for our guilt and iniquities; the chastisement [needful to obtain] peace and well being for us was upon Him, and with the stripes [that wounded] Him we are healed and made whole. (Isaiah 53:3-5) AMP

That it might be fulfilled which was spoken by Isaiah the Prophet, saying, "He Himself took our infirmities and bore our sicknesses" (Matthew 8:17) KJV

When evening came, they brought to Him many who were under the power of demons, and He drove out the spirits with a word and restored to health all who were sick. And thus He fulfilled what was spoken by the prophet Isaiah, He Himself took [in order to carry away] our weaknesses and infirmities and bore away our diseases. (Matthew 8:16-17) AMP

After this, Jesus knowing that all things were now accomplished that the scripture might be fulfilled, said, "I thirst". Now a vessel full of sour wine was sitting there; and they filled a sponge with sour wine, put it on hyssop and put it to His mouth. So when Jesus had received the sour wine. He said, "it is finished" and bowing His head, He gave up His spirit. (St: John 19:28-30)

<u>It's Already Done</u>

Chapter 1
Healing Belongs To You!

"It is your God given, blood bought right to live a good and healthy life".

Beloved, I pray that you may prosper in every way and [that your body] may keep well, even as [I know] your soul keeps well and prospers. (3 John 2 AMP)

God wants to heal you every where you hurt, **Spiritually, Emotionally, Physically, Socially, Mentally,** and **Financially.** God wants you well and Whole in every area of your life, **"Nothing Broken, Nothing Missing"**! God is our divine Healer, **(Yahweh-Rapha),** the Lord who heals, cures, repairs, mends, restores health. (Ex. 15:26).

God wants you to live a good and suitable life. He wants you to live a complete and full life. God wants you to prosper in every area of your life. Through the death and resurrection of His son Jesus Christ, God, the Father, made provision for your healing, freedom, protection, peace, joy, and deliverance from captivity. (Isaiah 53:4-5).

Jesus allowed Himself to be broken that through His brokenness He could Make you whole again. Don't forget to thank Him for what He has done. Many times, I've said, "Lord I sound like a broken record, saying this over and over again". The Lord responded with, "Stay right there, that's the problem, preachers mention healing in their sermons sometimes, but no one wants to stay on the subject long enough until the people get a revelation of the truth," "by whose stripes, We Were Healed" The subject of divine healing is a greatly neglected part of most people's Christianity; it is rarely even discussed in "mainstream" churches. Why? The primary reason for this neglect is that a very real Satan, the Devil has blinded the vast majority of humanity, including most professing Christians. Today, many church goers do not really study the subject of healing. They do not receive divine healing as real. They are content to follow the tradition of accepting sickness as a part of life, which is directly opposed to the word of God. We see much emotionalism in the church but very little genuine healing!

The day is coming when massive diseases will ravage the human race. Doctors and hospitals will be overwhelmed with the sick and dying. The doctors, (medical science), will have no answers or cures. But if we learn to trust God as our healer today, we can walk in divine health, even with the sick and diseased all around us.

It is our Dream, our Vision, God's Plan, God's Design, our Purpose, our Passion, our Privilege, our Call, our Destiny, to take the healing message of Jesus Christ to the Nations of the world..........Via......"Healing Explosion", Personal appearances, Video & Cassette tapes, Radio broadcasting, Television programming, and written materials. I've seen God work many miracles in my life and in the lives of many others that He has allowed us to minister to. After having two (2) near death experiences and many other healings in my body, and seeing my husband, (Pastor Brown) healed and completely restored from a crippling stroke, the Lord placed a burden on my heart for those people that are sick and hurting, suffering with all manner of spiritual, physical, emotional, mental and financial diseases.

After many years of wrestling in prayer, studying God's word, seeking the will of God for my life, God anointed, appointed, and commissioned me to go and **[set the captive free]**! "I want you to prepare a place for those whom nothing has been prepared." Saith the Lord! By the grace of God, we have conducted 34 healing explosions at the time of this writing. In the beginning, we called our meetings Healing Conferences, but after the conference in Atlanta Georgia, where the Healing power of God exploded like **DYNOMITE**, He gave us these words...**Healing Explosion!** God is sending a healing explosion to the Churches in America and around the world. Its time for God's people to have a life changing experience. This is the season of **Release and Recovery.** This is God's time of completion. God is releasing an anointing that will destroy every yoke and remove every burden. This is the time for God's **Healing Power** to **Explode** in our lives and bring change and healing to us on every level.

When the Tsunami took place in Asia, I was so overwhelmed by the impact of it, all the deaths and destruction. One night I was crying out to God for those people and that nation, and the Lord spoke to my spirit and said, (and I will write this with as much clarity as I can) "Warn my people to repent and prepare to move to higher ground. They said there was no warning about the tsunami, but, there was a warning, when the animals started acting out of character, sea birds lifting and flying to higher ground, elephants that had been staked out, pulled their stakes out of the ground and moved to higher ground, the sea started to recede, sky activity became weird, but the people paid no attention. They heeded not the warning, because they did not heed the warning, many people that could have been spared were swept away. If my people heed not my warning, just as the people were overtaken and swept away so will it be with my people.

There is an avalanche of healing coming to the body of Christ, struggling with sickness and disease will be a thing of the past. Just as the Tsunami rose out of the sea in Asia, there is a spiritual Tsunami that shall rise out of the sea of the Holy Ghost, and in this Tsunami, instead of destruction there shall be restoration, instead of death, there shall be life, more souls shall be swept into the kingdom of God in 3-6 months than has come into the kingdom in 35 years, healing shall take place on an unprecedented scale, missing limbs shall be restored, the blind shall see, the lame shall walk, women who have lost there breasts and other reproductive organs to cancer, etc., shall find themselves productive again, breasts shall be restored, missing limbs restored, eyeballs restored, AIDS, sickness and diseases will have no power, financial prosperity will know no end, even the dead shall be raised to life. But we (the Church) must repent and move to higher ground, God is calling us higher in our prayer life, higher in our relationship with Him, higher in our commitment, higher in our worship, our praise, a higher place of integrity and honor, a higher level of faithfulness, we must move up higher in our love walk, and above all we must move to a higher level of obedience. We must be quick to hear God and obey Him at all cost. We must surrender our will and our way to God.

God is releasing an anointing that the Body of Christ has yet to experience.

> (Therefore also now, saith the Lord (Fear not, O land, be glad and rejoice. For the Lord has done marvelous things! Do not be afraid, you beasts of the field. for the open pastures are springing up). And the tree bears its fruit, the fig tree and the vine yield their strength.
>
> Be glad the, ye children of Zion, and rejoice in the Lord your God; for He hath given you the former rain moderately, and he will cause to come down for you the rain, the former rain, and the latter rain in the first month.
>
> The threshing floors shall be full of wheat. And the vats shall overflow with new wine and oil. S I will restore to you the years that the swarming locust has eaten. The crawling locust; The consuming locust; And the chewing locust. My great Army which I sent among you.
>
> You shall eat in plenty and be satisfied. And praise the name of the Lord your God, who has dealt wondrously with you. And My people shall never be put to

shame. Then you shall know that I am in the midst of Israel. I am the Lord your God, And there is no other, My people shall never be put to shame. And it shall come to pass afterward, That I will pour out my spirit upon all flesh, Your sons and your daughters shall prophesy, Your old men shall dream dreams, Your young men shall see visions. (Joel 2:21-28).

In these passages we see **Repentance**, with **Repentance** comes **Revival**, with **Revival** comes **Restoration**, with **Restoration** comes, **Refreshing, Renewal, Recovery, Replenishing,** and **Rejuvenation**.

When I embarked on this journey of divine healing, I was battling with so many different types of sicknesses in my body. From the time I can remember, it seems like I was battling with some type of sickness or pain. The first real physical pain I can remember is, my left knee, the cartilage that keeps the bones from rubbing together, didn't work, my knee bones would rub together until sometimes it would slip out of joint, the pain was almost unbearable, for days I would have to walk as if I had an artificial leg, then there was the pain that came with my cycle, headaches, would get so bad that I would lose my sight, not to mention all of the emotional and mental pain that I endured over the years. There were times when I was so hurt and broken, I thought, if I could just put my hand in my chest and massage my heart, maybe I would feel better, but I couldn't, only God could remove this pain.

My entire life was a constant struggle; I would go off to myself and wonder about this God. If God is real and He loves me, why does He allow me to suffer this way? I grew up in a Christian home, but I had never heard about God's love or His healing power. O' yes, I knew there was a God, but, is he a good God, or is he the big bad wolf waiting to get me when I messed up? God was not spoken of openly like he is today, especially by the children, mention the name God; and you're in big trouble for using the Lord's name in vain.

My parents thought that hard work was the cure for everything, even curiosity about God. I love my parents, but I must keep it real. My parents, though they loved God, and maybe in their own way they loved me, but they never told me that they loved me, or that God loved me. There was no affection shown in our family, no arms to comfort when the cares of life became unbearable, but there was a lot of shouting and degradation, no encouragement to pursue your dreams, but there was plenty of assurance that we would never amount to anything. My parents never gave me the right to dream or hope for anything beyond the farm that we lived and worked on. We worked in the fields before we went to school and after we came from school, in between work, there was homework and every other chores that went along with farm life. My father insisted that we got good grades in school, but if any of us expressed an interest in anything other than a life on the farm, it got cut down before it could grow and bear any fruit.

My parents were serious farmers, some of the land they farmed were there own, but most of the land that we farmed belonged to other men that owned almost every piece of land within reach, men that didn't think as much of us as they did their farm animals, we sharecropped the land that was owned by the other, (rich) men, they treated us like slaves owned by the "Master", we did the work and they collected the money. My parents grew every type of crop that was available, cotton, tobacco, beans, watermelons, and a number of other things. There was never a rest period, we were working all the time, there seemed to be a crop for every season. There was little to no recreation or child's play, occasionally, we were allowed to go swimming in the nearby pond, or Maybe, once per year we went to a base ball game, although, my father Played on the neighborhood team every Saturday, while our father played base ball the children had to work in the fields. Then there was the once- a-year shopping spree. My father would load all of us on the back of the old T-Model pick up and drive us to the "dry good-grocery store", there we would be fitted for shoes, etc. All of the farmers in the area would go there to "trade", they got everything they needed. At the end of the year, when the crops were harvested and sold, they would go to "settle" their debts. It was a vicious cycle, each year the same thing, over and over, they never got out of debt. We barely survived while the store owners and the land owners grew richer.

It seemed like no matter how well we did a job, we would never hear "good job", just once I wanted to hear, "good job" or "you did good" their favorite quote was, "you will never be nothing, as long as you live you will never have nothing. "Well done, Daddy and Moma", it didn't matter how hot the sun got, or how bad your head hurt you're going to work the fields.

I grew up in a household of sixteen children. I am the eldest girl of the bunch, so I became the house maid. My mom had the babies, but I got the privilege of caring for them. I had to keep the babies and the house clean, wash the clothes, scrub the floors on my knees, sweep the yard, which was all dirt, no grass, do the ironing, "without spot or wrinkle". At eight years old I was standing in a chair making biscuits and cooking a five course meal for twelve people. During those days, after having a baby, the mother would stay in bed or inactive for six weeks. When I was twelve years old, I was sent to the fields to work until eleven O'clock, then I would have to go home and cook the mid day meal for the others, while the food was cooking, whatever needed to be done around the house, I had to get it done, sweep the yard, mop the floor, wash the clothes, etc. and have the food on the table when they got to the house.

Every year there was a new baby in our house. Every time a new baby came, I was taken out of the field for about six weeks only to become the fulltime house maid again! There were times in the Winter when I would wash the clothes, it was so cold, before I could remove my hands from hanging them on the line the clothes would be frozen stiff. My parents gave us the necessities of life, food, clothing, and shelter, but there was no show of love, no emotional support, no hope for a future, and, no prayer life or word foundation.

Every day it seemed like there was a new verbal or physical abuse for Something, like not putting enough water in a glass that my father asked for, or something crazier than that. I know, they did their best, but a child does not understand, when it seems like a punishment instead of a pleasure to be a member of their own family.

My strongest memory of growing up, was wishing that I would die before the next morning. I always thought that somehow, it had to be my fault that I was not loved like my siblings, cousins, or even the neighborhood children, my parents were always kind and understanding with them. I do not write this to offend any member of my family or to shed a bad light on my parents, because I'm sure they did the best they could with what they had, I only write this to bring glory to God.

Rejection and abuse of any kind is hard for a child, but it's a marvelous Thing when God turns it around for good. Please allow me to encourage you, no matter what kind of abuse you have suffered, or how miserable your childhood may have been, no matter what negative seeds has been sown into the ground of your life, God can take those negative seeds and turn them into a positive harvest. No matter where you are, or what your life is like right now, there is nothing, no part of your life that God cannot fix. God can take bad memories and turn them into good memories, if you will trust your life to him.

I'm beginning to realize, "no pain, no gain". All of the pain, struggles of Your life can be used by God to bring glory to Himself. God does not outright afflict us with sickness and disease, but, when Satan forms these and other types of weapons against us, God sees it as an opportunity to teach you spiritual strategies, and make something better out of you. I do not believe that God would allow you to be tempted or tried in any way, that he did not think that you were able to go through it victoriously. (No temptation has overtaken you, except such as is common to man: [Someone has gone through this and came out a winner, so can you], but God is faithful, who will not allow you to be tempted beyond what you are able, but with the temptation will also make a way of escape, [God will not leave you in any situation long enough for it to destroy you, He will get you out on time] that you may be able to bear it. (1 Corn: 10:13).

From the time I can remember, it seems like I was battling with some kind of sickness or pain. The first real pain I can remember, was in my left knee, the cartilage that keeps the bones from rubbing together didn't work, my knee bones would rub together until sometimes it would slip out of joint, the pain was almost unbearable, for days I would have to walk like I had an artificial leg. Then there was the pain that came once per month, the headaches would get so bad that I would lose my sight, not to mention all of the emotional and mental pain that I endured over the years.

I would often go off to myself and wonder, if God is real and He loves us, why would He allow people to suffer with pain, sickness and disease like I was suffering? I did not know that he had already carried my sicknesses and bore my infirmities and carried them away from me. **(Matthew 8:16-17).** I did not know that He was manifested to destroy the works of the devil. (1 John 3:8). I did not know that He came to Set the Captives FREE! So I begun to think that, if God is good and He loves me, then I must be bad? It must be my fault, I must really be bad and God is punishing me by letting me be sick all the time, of course this was not true, God is good!

I went to doctor after doctor, but it seemed like I would never get well. There was always one more doctor to see, one more new medicine to try, and I just grew worse. I came very close to losing my mind. I was very suicidal. I was very much like the woman with the issue of blood in (Matthew 8) I knew next to nothing about the healing power of God. I also ran out of money. But one day I heard a preacher named Kenneth Copeland on the radio talking about divine healing, I ordered the tapes he was offering on the program that day, when the tapes arrived, I begin playing them day and night. I kept the word going into my ear, I kept the word before my eyes, (Proverbs 4:20-27). I consumed the word with my spirit like we consume food with our mouth. When my heart (spirit) got fill with the word, the word came alive in my heart, and I begun to speak it out of my mouth, (by whose stripes, we were healed), I spoke God's word until every symptom of any sickness or disease was driven from my body. I came to know, **<u>God Wants Us Well and Whole, Nothing Broken, Nothing Missing!!!!</u>**

During all those years of battling with sickness and pain, I kept having these recurring dreams and visions of multitudes of people being healed of all manner of sicknesses and diseases, demonic oppression, etc. The strange thing about the dreams and visions, I would see myself, Teaching the Word of God and laying hands on the people as they were being healed. Of course, I couldn't understand that, I would think, something is wrong with this picture, if I could get anybody healed, it would be me. So I thought maybe, this is a part of being sick all the time. I did not know that I could be healed, until I had two (2) near death experiences. Note: (That which God will use you in the most, that's where you will be tried or tested most. The enemy fears that call that God have upon your life, so he tries his best to take you out before God can develop and use it).

SAVED AND STILL SICK

Even, after I accepted Jesus as my personal Lord and savior, I was still sick. I felt bad all the time, I had very little strength, I had very low self esteem, I thought about **suicide** almost all the time. I just got so tired of being sick, I got tired of myself, I wanted to die every day I was alive. When I gave my life to Jesus, I was filled with the Holy Spirit, but I had no revelation of God's Word; born again, filled with the Holy Spirit, but still sick. I went to church, but I was still sick, I prayed, but I was still sick. I found nothing at church but mostly man made religion and traditions. Not once did I ever hear anyone quote (Isaiah 53:4-5, or 1 Peter 2:24, or Matthew 8:16-17), not once did I hear anyone say, "with the stripes of Jesus, we are healed" I didn't know what I was looking for, but I knew it wasn't in the church, so I stopped going, because it was down right boring; "church was killing me"!

After hearing Kenneth Copeland talk about divine healing, I began listening to his tapes with scriptures about healing, I read every book that I could get my hands on, I fed the word of God into my spirit until my heart got impregnated with the word of God. The power of God's word began to expand on the inside of me. The more I poured the word into my spirit, the more it expanded, it began to fill my mind, it filled my heart, it filled my inner man until it began to fill my mouth and started spilling out into words, that overflowed to my body. God miraculously healed me from diabetes and a death threatening stomach ulcer. God is a good God, and God is healer.

If you have never been sick to the point of no hope of ever being well, you would not understand how grateful I am to God for healing me. Yes, I can truly say, "with the stripes of Jesus, I am Healed". God is my healer. At the time of this writing I had not been to a doctor in twenty two (22) years, God keeps my body healed and strong. I never tell people not to go to the doctor, because if you need a physician, then see one, but if you discover your heavenly physician, you will have little need of a medical physician. Then you can take the money that you have been giving the doctors and sow it into the kingdom of God. Its funny how we will spend thousands of $$ with the doctor trying to get cured, but when God heal us, we don't have the wisdom to bring Him an offering.

This is not to say that I don't get attacked by Satan with some sickness or disease. I get attacked almost everyday, but I know the truth, and the truth has made me free. I don't deny the attacks; I just deny Satan the right to park on God's property. There is no sickness, no disease that God cannot and will not heal; no matter what you're battling with right now, God is ready and willing to heal you, if you will trust Him as your healer. (St: Luke 5:12-14). **"For I am the God that healeth thee". (Exodus 15:26).** If God can heal me from all of the sicknesses, diseases and pain; (physical and emotional), surely He can heal you from your suffering. (Eph: 3:20, Mark 10:23-27).

God is Healer! Child of God, you have a God given right to partake in the healing provisions that the Father has provided for through His Son Jesus Christ. You have been raised up and made to sit in heavenly places with Christ Jesus; above all powers, principalities, all dominions, and thrones, all powers of darkness, including sickness and disease; Jesus already bore these for you, and you don't have to bear them any more. Jesus said; "Behold, I give you the authority to trample on serpents and scorpions, and over all the power of the enemy, and nothing shall by any mean hurt you" (St. Luke 10:19) Don't let Satan steal your heritage, don't let him impose his devices upon you, don't let him use fear to keep you in bondage to sickness, disease, and pain in your body and mind.

After the first near death experience, God told me to go and tell My people 'to get ready and stay ready, for my coming is sooner than any one thinks". After that, again God begun to visit me in dreams and visions about healing; Many times I would awake praising God, or weeping because the Spirit of the Lord was moving upon me. Almost every time this happened; God would give me these two scriptures; (Is: 6 & Jer.1). In between episodes, the Lord would lead me to (St: Luke 4:18-20, St: Mark 16:15-20, and many others). At the same time there was so much unrest in my spirit; and turmoil in my life, every thing got on my nerves; I wasn't sure who was pulling at me, am I being visited by God, the Devil or who?

One day, around eleven o'clock, I was sweeping my living room floor, suddenly, there was a light flooding through my glass door, I couldn't bear to look into the light with my naked eyes, so I put my hands up to protect my eyes, thinking, what in the name of Jesus is this? When my eyes adjusted to the light, I could see the form of a man standing in the light, yet he was the light. It was as if he stepped right through the glass door, next thing I knew he's standing in the middle of my living room and I'm standing face to face with the King of Glory. OH' Lord help me, I am so unworthy!!! The Lord visited me in an open vision that day, He showed me many things, some I can share and some I cannot share. That day, Jesus placed two bottles of oil in my hands, He said, "these are yours, go, take my word and set the captive free, go lay hands on the sick and they shall be healed and recover from all manner of diseases" . That day, he showed me people with every imaginable disease, waiting in line to be prayed for.

My message to you is not profound or complicated, its very simple. **GOD WANTS YOU WELL AND WHOLE, NOTHING BROKEN, NOTHING MISSING!!** God wants you to prosper in every area of your life, God wants to heal you every where you hurt. Now is the time for God's people to experience the fullness of God, and walk in total wellness and wholeness. Its time to declare; **"GOD IS HEALER"._**

Chapter 2
Redemption

> Christ has redeemed us from the curse of the law, having become a curse for us, (for it is written, cursed is everyone who hangs on a tree) (Gal; 3:13)

As the story goes, Satan came to Eve, Adam's wife, in the form of a serpent and deceived her into disobeying God. Adam, although he was not deceived, went along with it. When Satan came into the garden that day, he was powerless, he had no power at all, he had to disguise himself and come in like a snake, he didn't even talk to Adam, he talked to his wife. Now, Adam was standing right there, he should have used his authority and kicked the devil out right then, but he did not, instead, he set aside the command God gave him and did what Satan told him to do. When he did that he died to God and made Satan his lord.

In bowing his knee to Satan, he gave Satan authority over all that God had given him, he made Satan illegitimate ruler of this world, immediately, things changed. Through one man's sin, the kingdom of darkness came into power, death, sickness, disease, infirmities, poverty and lack passed to all men. The earth and everything in it was suddenly cursed. OK, you say, are we to live under this curse for the rest of our lives? Wasn't there anything God could do?

Yes, God could do something, and he did. He sent Jesus, through Jesus, He redeemed you, He set you free from the curse. The moment you made Jesus Lord of your life, you were delivered from the lordship of Satan. You were redeemed from the curse of sickness, pain, diseases, physical pain and suffering, infirmities, lack, poverty, and even death.

1. Redemption: redemption is recovery of something pawned or mortgaged.
2. Payment of an obligation

    3. Deliverance upon payment of ransom
    4. To be brought back to your original state
    5. Salvation from sin through Christ's sacrifice.

When Adam disobeyed God and bowed his knees to Satan, he gave Satan a mortgage over the entire human race, he gave Satan the right to hold you hostage until the ransom was paid. But it didn't stop there, Jesus came, paid the ransom, He paid off your mortgage, through His death and resurrection. He paid the price to release you from sin, sickness, diseases, bondage, fear, oppression, and everything in the kingdom of darkness. Don't let Satan deceive you, he lost his rights to hold you hostage, he lost his right to hold you in captivity.

> (Let the redeemed of the Lord say so, whom He has redeemed from the hand of the enemy). (PS. 107:20)
>
> (Giving thanks to the father, who has qualified us to be partakers of the inheritance of the saints in the light; (qualified us), qualified mean primarily to make competent or sufficient, and secondarily, to entitle, authorized, or enable.) (Col: 1:12)
>
> Who also made us sufficient as ministers of the New Covenant. Not of the letter but of the Spirit; for the letter kills; but the Spirit gives life.)

Just as God honored Israel by giving that nation Canaan as an earthly allotment, so He has honored each member of the Church, (body of Christ) with the potential of obtaining the inheritance of Spiritual Canaan

> He has delivered us from the power of darkness and conveyed; (transferred) us into the kingdom of the Son of His love. In whom we have redemption through His blood, the forgiveness of sins. (Colossians 1:13-14)

Delivered us................from darkness, conveys the idea of Salvation rescuing us from the powers of darkness, it includes rescue from such negatives as danger, (spiritual and temporal), death, sickness, disease, and hostile situations in general. (Ps: 33:18-19. Behold, the eye of the Lord is on those who fear Him, on those who hope in His mercy, to deliver their soul from death, and to keep them alive in famine). These rescues, include both present deliverance and future. Conveyed, refers to the deportation of captured armies or populations from one Country to another.

> Thus, you were circumcised with a circumcision not made with hands, but in a (spiritual) circumcision [performed by] Christ, by striping off the body of the flesh (the whole corrupt, carnal nature with it's passions and lusts). you were dead, [Christ], having [freely] forgiven us all our transgressions. Having cancelled and blotted out and wiped away the handwriting of the note [bond] with its legal decrees and demands which was in force and stood against us

> [hostile to us] This [note with its regulations, decrees, and demands]. He set aside and cleared completely out of our way by nailing it to [His] cross. [God disarmed the principalities and powers that were ranged against us and made a bold display and public example of them, in triumphing over them in Him and in it [the cross] (Colossians 2:11-15 AMP)
>
> In Him we have redemption (deliverance and salvation) through His blood, the remission (forgiveness) of our offenses (shortcomings and trespasses), in accordance with the riches and the generosity of His gracious favor. (Ephesians:!:7 AMP).
>
> When He ascended on high, He led captivity captive, and gave gifts unto men. (Eph: 4:8)
>
> Therefore it is said, when He ascended on high, He led captivity captive (He led a train of vanquished foes) and He bestowed gifts on men. (Ephesians: 4:8 AMP).

Child of God, you have been redeemed, you don't have to bow beneath the burden of sickness and disease; Christ has redeemed, (rescued), (translated), (transferred) you out of the hand of the enemy.

Surely He has borne our griefs (sickness and disease), and carried our sorrows (pains). To be our perfect High Priest, Christ Jesus had to know our griefs by experience. Since a High Priest must be one with the people in order to represent them, the incarnation was indispensable to the atoning work of Christ.

Has borne…..Carried: These verbs mean "to take upon ones self," or "to carry as a burden,"

> But He was wounded for our transgressions, He was bruised for our iniquities, the chastisement of our peace was upon Him, and with His stripes you are healed. (IS. 53:4-5).
>
> Who His own self bore our sins in His own body on the tree, that we, being dead to sins should live unto righteousness; by whose stripes, "We Were Healed"'. (1 Peter 2:24).
>
> When evening came, they brought to Him many who were under the powers of demons, and He drove out the spirits with a word and restored to health all who were sick. And thus He fulfilled what was spoken by the Prophet Isaiah, "He himself took (in order to carry away our weaknesses and infirmities and bore away our diseases. (Matthew 8:16-17 AMP).

There is no doubt that healing for the body, the mind, and every part of our lives is provided in the same redemption as salvation is for the spirit. In redemption, there is physical, mental, social, financial, and spiritual healing. When Jesus is present in your life, the power to save, deliver, and heal, is inside of you.

For us to live in the manner Jesus intended for us to live, we must have a revelation of,

WHO JESUS IS?

Before the coming of Christ, God dealt with His people (as told in the Old Testament) with examples (pictures) that would be explained or fulfilled in the New Testament, such as; Sin entered into the world through the eating of the fruit of a tree by a woman being deceived by Satan. Jesus, the remedy for sin, came into the world through a woman and died on a tree, (Acts 13:29).

"They took him down from the tree, and laid him in a sepulcher. God said to Moses, "Thou shalt say unto the children of Israel, I AM hath sent me unto you. (Exodus 3:14).

In the New Testament Jesus said, "I say unto you, before Abraham was, **I AM,**" (Jn. 8:58) and then he finished the sentence: " I AM the **WAY** the **TRUTH,** and the **LIFE**. (Jn. 14:6), **I AM the DOOR,** (JN. 10:7)

I AM the **GOOD SHEPHERD.** (Jn. 10:14) **I AM the VINE.** (Jn. 15:5) **I AM the RESURRECTION**. (Jn. 11:25).

God gave ten commandments (the law) **50 days** after the first **Passover** (O.T.) The outpouring of the Holy Spirit was **50 days** after the resurrection of the **Passover Lamb.**

In the Old Testament, the priest offered the daily sacrifices, not only for the people, for himself; also because he was not perfect and had infirmities. (Hebrews 5:2,3).

The Holy of Holies, where resided the Ark of the Covenant, was separated from the rest of the Tabernacle by a veil. Once a year the high priest entered alone to offer the blood for himself and for the sins of the people. (Hebrews 9:9).

Jesus, who was with the Father from the beginning, "took upon Himself the form of man" to become the sacrifice and then our **HIGH PRIEST.**

> Jn. 6:38 For I come down from heaven, not to do mine own will, but the will of him that sent me.
>
> Jn. 17:4,5,24 I have glorified thee on the earth. I have finished the work which thou gives me to do. And now, O Father, glorify thou me, with thine own self with the glory which I had with thee **BEFORE THE WORLD WAS.**
>
> Jn. 19:17 And he bearing his cross went forth into a place called the place of a skull...where they crucified him.
>
> Hebrews 9:28 So Christ was once offered to bear the sins of many.

> Hebrews 10:14; For by one offering he hath perfected for ever them that are sanctified.
>
> Matt. 27:50,51 Jesus, when he had cried again with a loud voice, yielded up the ghost, And, behold, the veil of the temple was rent in twain from the top to the bottom.
>
> Hebrews 9:24,10,12 For Christ is not entered into the Holy places made with hands, but into heaven itself, now to appear in the presence of God for us...after he had offered one sacrifice for sins for ever, set down at the right hand of God.

When God rent the veil of the temple from the TOP to the BOTTOM, he abolished the separation between the two places. It was His invitation to the people (all people) to enter and present their petitions directly to Him without a human intermediary.

> 1 Tim. 2:5,6, For there is one God, and one mediator between God and man, the man called Christ Jesus; who gave himself a ransom for all.
>
> Hebrews 4:15,16 For we have not a high priest which cannot be touched with the feeling of our infirmities; but was in all points tempted like as we are, yet without sin. Let us therefore come boldly unto the throne of grace, that we may obtain mercy, and find grace to help in time of need.
>
> Hebrews 7:25 Wherefore he is able also to save them to the uttermost that come unto God by him, seeing he ever liveth to make intercession for them.

God made the receiving of His salvation so SIMPLE THAT EVEN A CHILD can UNDERSTAND. It involves only the individual and Himself so that anyone, regardless of location or circumstances, (drowning, lost in the desert, dying on a battlefield, etc.) could call upon Him in the name of His Son and be saved.

> Acts 2:21 Whosoever shall call on the name of the Lord shall be saved.

Perhaps you think you are not worthy of going directly to Jesus or the Father with your petition.

> Ecc. 7:20 For there is not a just man upon earth, that doeth good, and sinneth not.
>
> Jn. 14:6 No man cometh unto the Father, but by me.
>
> Jn. 16:37 Him that cometh to me I will in no wise cast out.
>
> Jn. 16:23,24 Whatsoever ye shall ask the Father in my name, he will give it you...ask, and ye shall receive, that your joy may be full.
>
> Hebrews 13:15 By him therefore let us offer the

sacrifice of praise to God continually, that is the fruit of our lips giving thanks to his name.

Jesus is Lord! (Yahweh/Jehovah), His name is above every name in heaven and earth and beneath the earth, (Philippians 2:8-11). Jesus is Healer, Jesus is Savior, Jesus is, **"The Lord Will Provide"** (**Jehovah-Jireh**), Jesus is Protector, Jesus is, **"The Lord Is Our Righteousness"** (**Jehovah-Tsidqenu**), Jesus is our Peace, Jesus is **I AM THAT I AM (The self-sufficient God)**, Jesus is (**Jehovah-Elohim**), the Lord is God, Jesus is, **The Lord God Most High, (Jehovah-Elyon);** "possessor of heaven and earth", **"the Deliverer"**, Jesus is The Almighty God (**El-Shaddai**), "the breasty one, our eternal source of sufficient supply ", Jesus is our healer, **"The Lord Is Healer…..(Jehovah-Repheka),** and the list goes on.

SALVATION!

"That if you confess with your mouth the Lord Jesus
and believe in your heart that God raised him from
the dead, you will be saved". (Rom: 10:9)

We must realize that Salvation is more than just the means to miss hell and go to heaven. Salvation is the saving of a man from the power and effects from sin, liberation from clinging to the phenomenal world of appearance, and final union with ultimate reality. The realization of the supremacy of infinite mind over all, bringing with it the destruction of the illusion of sin, sickness and death. Yes, heaven is the ultimate goal, but, you must die to go to heaven, meanwhile we must l ive. We must be saved. **SALVATION-SOTERIA………**denotes: The saving of man from the power and effects from sin.

Liberation from clinging to the phenomenal world of appearance and final union with ultimate reality. The realization of the supremacy of infinite mind over all bringing with it the destruction of the illusion of sin, sickness, and death. Preservation from destruction or failure, deliverance from danger, difficulty and apprehension, spiritual and eternal deliverance. Salvation is to be freed from the bondage of sin. The agent or means or course of spiritual experience, determining the soul's redemption.

PRESERVATION is to keep safe from injury or peril; to guard; to keep or maintain in tact; to protect; to prevent; (organic bodies from decaying). Salvation keeps us from decaying, like salt keeps meat from rotting.

"We are seated with Him in heavenly places,
(Ephesians 2:5-6).

You are a chosen generation (1 Peter 2:9), We are
more than conquerors, through Him who loved us".
(Romans 8:37).

Satan is not the super bad victor that he would like you to believe he is. Satan is a liar and a deceiver, he has no dominion over you, you are not his victim, you are the victor. When you know that healing is a vital part of your Salvation, you will no longer have a need for people to lay hands on you, you will no longer seek healing, because you know this is something you already possess. You know that you are redeemed from sickness and disease. When you know this, sickness and disease will no longer pose a threat to you. Then you will begin to see sickness and disease like the Hebrew boys saw the threat of the fiery furnace.

"Shadrach, Meshach, and Abednego answered and said to the king, O Nebuchadnezzar, we have no need to answer you in this matter, if that be the case, our God whom we serve is able to deliver us from the burning fiery furnace, and He will deliver us from your hand, O King. But if not, let it be known to you, O King, that we do not serve you gods, nor will we worship the golden image which you have set up". (Daniel 3:16-18).

"And the satraps, administrators, governors, and the King's counselors gathered together, and they saw these men on whose bodies the fire had no power; the hair of their head was not singed nor were their garments affected, and the smell of fire was not on them". (Daniel 3:22).

When you know that Jesus became your substitute, and was made sick so that you can be healed, you will know that sickness and disease can have no more effect on you than the fiery furnace had on the Hebrew boys. Your sickness as well as your sins were laid on Jesus on the cross. He bore our sicknesses and infirmities, therefore, we no longer need to bear them, with the stripes of Jesus, "We Were Healed".

In this writing, I find it necessary to keep repeating myself because I must drive this very important point to home, I must get this to sink in. We need not bare or suffer sicknesses, diseases, infirmities, oppression, depression, lack, poverty, or any thing that comes out of the realm of darkness, Jesus already suffered these things for us. Now we can arise in our faith and receive this complete work of salvation and redemption, our sins are forgiven and by the stripes of Jesus, **We Were Healed!**

This must become a revelation to the body of Christ. We have jumped, hollered and squalled about it long enough, now its time to walk in it. Its time to stand and declare, that "God is our healer", and we will no longer put up with the devil's mess.

Now! We are liberated from the hand of the oppressor, body, soul and spirit, we are free!! We have been rescued. You have been bought with a price; therefore glorify God in your body, and your spirit, which belongs to God. (1 Corn: 6:20). Jesus Christ, the Lord of our salvation, has fought, and won the battle, and set us free, from the power and dominion of Satan. Now you can say, "I am saved by grace, and through His blood, I have redemption, and by His stripes, "I am healed, I am redeemed". Satan is your enemy. Demons are your enemies. They hate you, they resent your legal rights to power over them. They will always seek to hinder your progress and cheat you out of everything that is promised to you. They will use every thing they can, fear, stress, pain, sickness, disease, financial problems, marital problems, they will use your spouse, your children, Government authority, threats of many kinds. But you must not allow fear to control you, you must rise up in the name of Jesus and take possession of the land. You must recognize your enemy.

> (Deut: 13:1-11), verses 8-10, "**You shall not consent to him or listen to him, nor shall your eye pity him, nor shall you spare or conceal him, but you shall surely kill him. Your hand shall be first against him to put him to death, and afterward the hand of all the people. And you shall stone him with stones until he dies, because he sought to entice you away from the Lord your God, who brought you out of the land of Egypt, (bondage), from the house of bondage.**

When the Lord led me to these words through his prophet, He said, "you must fight anything that would try to entice you to even consider going back to the house of bondage. Anything that would try to hinder you from entering into the abundance that Jesus came to give you, "KILL IT"….. Then he begun to show me in my spirit's mind, a serial killer does not kill at random, he kills by purpose, plan and strategy. He locates or scopes out his target (victim), he studies his victim's habits, routine, strength, weaknesses, skills and how he operates. He stalks his target until he gets him in a position where he can overpower him, he takes him captive, violates him, kills and dispose of him.

Anything that is trying to destroy your health, your peace of mind, your family life, your joy, your children, your financial security, your physical or spiritual safety, you must locate it, find the root of the culprit and KILL IT!!!!!! Pick up the rock of the word of God and stone it to death. Move from the defensive to the offensive, drive it out, pursue it until it dies. Pick up your weapons of warfare and begin to fight the good fight of faith.

> "**For the weapons of our warfare are not carnal, but mighty in God for the pulling down of strongholds. Casting down arguments and every high thing that exalts itself against the knowledge of God, bring every thought into captivity to the obedience of Christ.**

Our warfare is not against flesh and blood. (Eph. 6:12), therefore, carnal (weak, worldly, human, man made) weapons will not work. We need weapons that are God-empowered, (mighty in God). Their purpose is for pulling down (demolishing) strongholds, (anything opposing the will of God) (God's word), I believe the writer is referring strongly to the warfare of the mind, against arrogant, rebellious ideal and attitudes (which he call arguments) and against every high thing (pride) opposed to the true knowledge of God. The aim is to bring every disobedient thought into obedience to Christ. Make everything bow in submission, shut-up and listen to what the word has to say. God's word is the final authority, God has the last say! We must become skilled in the word of God and prayer. Everything evil, destructive, discouraging, malicious and binding is from Satan.

Everything good comes from God. (James 1:17,** 2 Peter 1:3,* * Luke 9:56). It is Satan's job to challenge your faith, Satan will rebel against you until the day you die, but don't let him win. Many people seem to think that God chooses to lay sickness and disease on them to teach them something, if this is true, then it must be God's will for you to be sick? Then why are you going to the doctor, taking medicine and doing everything you can to feel better and get well? Do you want to be out of the will of God? Some say, "maybe it's a blessing in disguise" but Jesus came to destroy the works of Satan, (1 John 3:8), which includes sickness and disease Don't fall for these lies, it is God's will for you to be well and whole, nothing broken and nothing missing. Through His blood we have redemption, and with the stripes that wounded Him, "We Were Healed"!!!

Chapter 3
Healing For You Today

Some strongly argue that divine healing is not for today, they say, divine healing went out with the apostles. (Psalm 107:20) Says, "He sent His word and healed them." The word is still very much around and its very much for you today. **(Exodus 15:26)," I am the Lord who heals you".** The Lord who heals you, Hebrew is Yahweh-Ropheka. This is one of the blessings enjoyed when one is in covenant relationship with God. Heals, Rapha (Rah-phah); to cure, heal, to mend, to restore to health or soundness; to restore to spiritual, mental, emotional, physical, social, and financial wholeness. Rophe: One who heals.

The main idea of the verb Rapha is physical healing. Some have tried to explain away the biblical teachings of divine healing, but all can see that this verse speaks of physical diseases and divine cure. This verse is widely referred to as the O.T. covenant of healing. It is called a covenant because in it God promises He will keep His people free from disease, and conditions the promise upon their diligent obedience. Our obedience to God's word brings His unlimited blessings upon our lives.

The word used here for "disease" (Hebrew-Makhaleh) and heals (Hebrew- Rapha), are regularly used for physical sickness and bodily healng. This is not just a spiritual concept, but also an intensely physical one. The covenant is made absolutely certain by the fact that God joins His mighty name to the promise, calling Himself "Yahweh-Rapha", meaning, "The Lord Who heals", Yahweh-Rapha is one of the compound names by which God revealed His attributes to Israel, here, His very name declares that it is His nature to be a healer to those who obey His word, to recover to health and keep them in good health. (**3 John 2, PS. 103:1-5, PS. 107:20).**

Healing is for you today. God wants you to be well, whole, sound, in good health and prosper in every area of your life. God wants you to have super-abundance on every level (1 Corn. 2:9), and He is willing and ready to heal you every where you hurt and bring you into the abundance He keeps ready for you. No matter where you are or what you're struggling with in life right now, pain, sickness, disease, infirmities, (physical or spiritual), heartaches, financial burdens, marital problems, depression, oppression, stress, a habit you can't seem to break, or just plain sick and tired of being sick and tired, the struggling can stop today. The power of God is available to heal you right now, today! The word is nigh thee, even in your mouth. (Rom. 10:8) Jesus came to give you life and that more abundantly. (John 10:10). Not just ordinary life, barely existing, barely getting by on need-more-street, struggling on -barely-make-it avenue, visiting the park-of-not-enough, sitting on the bench of lack, trying to climb poverty mountain. God wants you to live on abundant-boulevard. Your heavenly Father wants you to have His best, which He provided for you through the death and resurrection of His son, Jesus Christ. Check out your covenant, you have the right to abundance; you have the God given right to good health, wholeness and prosperity. Don't allow the enemy to steal your inheritance another day, step out of that barely- make-it mindset and step up into God's abundance, where there is more than enough. Make up your mind and begin to confess the promises of God. (Joshua 1:8) Declare, "I will not tolerate less than God's best." Say it until you believe and see it manifested in your life. (Mark 11:23).

Chapter 4
God Has Qualified You!

God has qualified you, He has equipped you, He has armed you. God Has made you fit, He has given you the power, the right to partake in the provision of His promises.

> "But as many as received Him, He gave the right (power) to become children of God, to those who believed on His name." (St. John 1:12).

> "For you are all sons of God through faith in Christ Jesus. For as many of you as were baptized into Christ have put on Christ. There is neither Jew nor Greek, there is neither slave nor free, there is neither male nor female, for you are all one in Christ Jesus. And if you are Christ's, then you are Abraham's seed, and heirs according to the promise." (Galatians 3:26-29, Genesis 12:1-3).

God has given you Exousia (ex-oo-see-ah); One of the four power words, (Dunamis, Exousia, Ischus, and Kratos). Exousia means authority or right to act, ability, privilege, capacity, delegated authority. Jesus had the Exousia to forgive sin, heal sickness, and cast out devils. Exousia is the right to use Dunamis, "might" Jesus gave His followers Exousia to preach, teach, heal, and deliver, and that authority has never been taken away (John 14:12), powerless ministries become powerful upon discovering the Exousia power resident in the name of Jesus and the blood of Jesus.

> "Giving thanks to the Father who has qualified us to be partakers of the inheritance of the saints in the light, He has delivered us from the power of darkness and conveyed us into the kingdom of the son of His love, in whom we have redemption through His blood, the forgiveness of sins. (Col. 1:12-14)

> Who also made us sufficient as ministers of the New Covenant, not of the letter, but of the spirit,. For the letter kills but the spirit gives life. (2 Corn. 3:6).
>
> (It is He) who has qualified us, (making us to be fit and worthy and sufficient), as ministers and dispenses of a New Covenant of salvation through Christ; not (ministers) of the letter (of legally written code) but of the spirit, for the code (of the law) kills, but the (Holy) Spirit makes alive. (2 Corn. 3:6 amp).

Qualified means primarily to make competent or sufficient, and secondarily, to entitle, authorize, or enable. God, the Father has made you unlimited, suitable, capable; adequate for the stipulated purpose; you are sufficient.

Just as God honored Israel by giving that nation Cannon as an earthly allotment, so has He honored each member of the Church with the potential of obtaining the inheritance of Heaven on earth?

> **He has delivered us from the Power of darkness and conveyed us into the Kingdom of the son of His love. (Col.1:13).**

Delivered us from darkness, gives us a picture of salvation rescuing us from the destruction of darkness. It includes a rescue from such things as danger, death, sickness and hostile situations in general.

> **"Behold the eye of the Lord is on those who fear Him. On those who hope in His mercy. To deliver their soul from death, and to keep them alive in famine". (Ps. 33:18-19).**

These rescues include both present deliverance and future, consummated deliverance in the world to come. Conveyed refers to the deportation or transference of captured armies or populations from one Country to another. Through the blood of Jesus you have been transferred [taken] out of the Kingdom of darkness, and placed in the Kingdom of light. Your name has been written in the Lamb's book of life. (St. Luke 10:17-20). Because your name is written in the Lamb's book of life, because your citizenship is now in heaven, (Phil. 3:20), you have been qualified, you have been authorized, you have been empowered to subdue the Kingdom of darkness, in the name of Jesus. You have the power to defeat and overcome every attack of the enemy in your life, your mind, your spirit, your body, your finances, your emotions, and your social life.

When you realize as a truth, you have been given power over Satan in the name of Jesus, by the blood and the word, you will no longer allow Satan to torment you and keep you in bondage to sickness, disease, infirmities, financial lack, depression, oppression, and stress. You will rise up in your faith and take control over every situation in your life.

When you fully realize that, you are no longer under the curse, (Gal. 3:13) Christ has redeemed you from the curse and anything that is a part of that curse, sickness, disease, infirmities, poverty, sorrow, grief, pain, and even death. You will no longer tolerate or put up with it.

Chapter 5
Healed By The Power Of God

There was a time in my life when I suffered some type of sickness, pain or stress everyday. Migraine headaches, hernias, excruciating pain in my knees and stomach, tonsillitis, allergies, diabetes, and the list goes on, you name it and I would get it. I grew up in a Christian home, but I knew nothing about the healing power of God. As I begun to study the word of God and discovered, Christ has redeemed me from the curse of the law. He already bore these things for me, and carried them away from me.

(IS. 53:4-5––Matthew 8:16-17) I no longer have to put up with or participate in sickness and disease. It is God's will for me to be well, whole and prosperous. (1John 2, St. John 10:10). I begun to apply (by faith), the word of God to my life, and today, I continue to do the same things, because it takes the same word that got me healed to keep me healed.

I will not mislead you, it did not happen instantly or quickly, it took perseverance, persistence, patient, consistency, longsuffering, endurance, speaking the word of God over my life all the time, watching what I said with my mouth, watching what I put in my body, not allowing others to sow negative seeds into my life, taking authority over every thought, when I just wanted to die. I did not give up! I had to believe the word when I did not believe that I could get well. There were many times when I didn't believe that I could believe, however, **(Faith cometh by hearing, and hearing by the word of God. (Rom. 10:17).**

I would ask the Holy Spirit to help me believe. I would speak the word until faith ignite in my heart and give me strength to get through another day, sometimes another hour, another minute, another second, some days seemed longer than others, but with each day of applying the word to my life, there was progress, until finally, every trace of sickness and disease was gone from my body. I no longer worry or become stressed out over the many sides of life. To God be the glory. Jesus is my Savior, my Banner, my Healer, my Fortress, He is my life. I praise the Lord for His goodness. God wants us well and whole. He wants to heal you everywhere you hurt, right now! Trust God, believe that He loves you and wants you well. Believe His word, stand on His word, speak His word, make the word of God your final Authority in everything. Don't be moved by anything but God's word.

> "While we do not look at the things which are seen, but at the things which are not seen. For the things which are seen are temporary, but the things which are not seen are eternal." (2 Corinthians 4:18).

You have a right to have the promises of God fulfilled in your life. You deserve to be well and whole. You deserve to prosper and have abundance. Through the death and resurrection of Jesus Christ, you have been given not only the right and means to live a Holy life, but to live a whole and prosperous life. You have the God-given right to live a healthy, prosperous full and complete life.

> "Beloved, I wish above all things that thou mayest prosper and be in health, even as thy soul prospers". (3 John 2).

God wants you well and whole, God wants you to prosper in every aspect of your life, not just your spiritual life, but every area. God wants you to live well and prosper, Health, [hugiaino]-[hoog-ee-ahee-no]; compare "hygiene" and "hygienic," to be sound in body, in good health.

GOD'S PROSPERITY: It is clear that God wants His children to prosper, how can we deny it? However, prosperity should not be the end in itself. It ought to be the result of a quality life, commitment, dedication, and action that is in line with God's word. In this text the word "prosper" (Greek-euodoo) literally means "to help on the road" or succeed in reaching," It clearly implies that divine prosperity is not a momentary, passing phenomenon, but rather it is an ongoing, progressive state of success and well-being. It is intended for every area of our lives; the spiritual, the physical and emotional, and the material. However, God does not want us to unduly emphasize any one area. We must maintain a balance.

Chapter 6
Ready For War

If you are going to war against an opponent, you would be very foolish not to sit down and count up the cost, and see whether you are able to meet him that comes against you with what you have. No one should enter battle without a careful examination of his or her resources and carefully planned battle strategies. As you study this book along side the bible and other faith building tools, you will learn some spiritual strategies for divine healing. It will also lead you to physical, mental, emotional, and spiritual healing and prepare you to minister God's healing power to others. It will lead you into proof-producing ministry. To be ready for war, we must have the proper ammunition and armor. In the 6th chapter of Ephesians, the apostle Paul instructs us to put on the whole armor of God.

> "Finally, my brethren, be strong in the Lord and in the power of His might. Put on the whole armor of God, that you may be able to stand against the wiles of the devil". (Ephesians 6:10-11).

The apostle Paul admonishes us to put on the whole armor of God in order to stand against the forces of hell. It is clear that our warfare is not against physical forces, but against invisible powers who have clearly defined levels of authority in a real, though invisible sphere of activity. Paul, however, not only warns us of a clearly defined structure in the invisible realm, he instructs us to take up the whole armor of God in order to maintain a "battle stance" against this unseen satanic structure. All of this armor is not just a passive protector in facing the enemy it is to be used offensively against these satanic forces. You shouldn't be running from devils, you should be running after them) Praying always with all prayer and supplication in the spirit. When Jesus commissioned anyone to preach the gospel, he also commands them to minister healing and deliverance. He told them, "as you go, heal the sick, cast out demons", (Matthew 10:1,7,8). When he went back to the Father he gave believers a great responsibility to take the gospel to all people. "Go ye into all the world, and preach the gospel to every creature". (Mark 16:15). You cannot fulfill responsibility without authority. Jesus also gave believers the authority to fulfill the responsibility. That authority, Jesus also gave believers the abilities to fulfill the responsibility. That authority includes power over all the power of the enemy. (St. Luke 10:18-19).

"And these signs shall follow them that believe; in my name shall they cast out devils, they shall lay hands on the sick and they shall recover." (Mark 16:17-18).

Are you ready to pick up your spiritual armor and fight your way out of a life of sickness and disease, out of a life of bondage, out of a life of poverty and lack, out of a life of depression and oppression, and step into a life of victory in Jesus Christ? Are you ready to be healed by the power of God? Are you ready to do battle for your physical body? Do you want to see the sick healed and made whole and those that are in bondage set free?

If you are a believer, then you must answer the call to arms. As you approach the subject of healing and deliverance, always remember that physical healing is secondary to spiritual reconciliation through Jesus Christ, which is the greatest miracle of healing. Healing is the children's bread, don't settle for crumbs!

As you embark on this journey of healing, make the decision to disregard past experiences and traditions you have been taught. Do not seek formulas and methods to receive or minister healing. The bible gives no special formulas, although various principles are revealed, instead of seeking formulas; understand that the healer is within you. Seek to increase your knowledge of an intimate relationship with Him. Jesus and the Holy Spirit are resident within. Healing is not something you seek from the outside, but something you learn to release from the inside. You are only to understand principles that will help you to release the power within you. Don't spend your time trying to explain unanswered questions, you are not called for that, you are called to believe the word of God. You are simply called to minister Salvation and healing, and leave the results with God. God will perform His word.

Jesus is the same yesterday, and today, and forever. (Hebrews 13:8). The same powerful, life-giving Spirit that was released to open the eyes of the blind and heal the sick through Jesus Christ, is still working within you today. The word of God never changes. It is just as powerful today as it was when Jesus walked the earth and released words of healing and deliverance. The words that Jesus spoke were full of the life of God. Jesus said, "The words that I speak to you, they are spirit and they are life". (St. John 6:63). "For the word of God is living and powerful, and sharper than any two-edged sword, (Hebrews 4:12), God's word is still filled with life- giving power, and where God's word is dominate, the power of God is available to heal. Jesus said, "Heaven and earth shall pass away, but my words shall not pass away" (Matthew 24:35), claim the promises of God by faith, and act on them, believing God's healing power to be released, you will be healed. That same life-giving Spirit who raised Jesus from the dead is still working in the earth today. Regardless of the devastating circumstances you may be facing, the symptoms of disease in your body, the report you have received from your doctor. God word declares that all things are possible with God and him who believes. There is healing in the written and the living word of God, "He sent His word and healed them and delivered them from their destruction. (PS. 107:20) Isaiah spoke and said;

> "So shall my word be that goeth forth out of my mouth, it shall not return unto me void, but it shall accomplish that which I please, and prosper in the things whereto I sent it" (Isaiah 55:11)

There is a stream of God's divine healing power flowing from the throne of God to heal every sickness and every disease afflicting mankind today. A flow of God's divine healing power has been released to heal leukemia, heart disease, arthritis, multiple sclerosis, cancer, emphysema, diabetes, lung disorder, AIDS, blood disease, skin diseases, and disorders, and every other disease, to remove growths and tumors, open blind eyes, restore hearing to the deaf, heal diseased limbs, cause the lame and paralyzed to walk, cast out demons, and restore missing limbs, organs and parts, and restore people to sound minds and health.

Beyond any doubt in my mind, God wants you well and whole, nothing broken, and nothing missing. God's word reveals that it is His will to Heal you. If you have any doubts, check the quick reference page following this chapter, then flip through your bible and read the scriptures.

God has made full provision for our healing. He stands ready to heal you right now. There is absolutely no sickness, no disease, no physical or mental affliction that God cannot or will not heal. It is my prayer that the things that are written in this book will raise your faith to heights that will minister healing and deliverance to every part of your life. I am not a healer, I am just a person sharing the love of God with you, God is the healer. I am only a vessel which God chose to flow through an out to....

....People who are hurting and in pain.
....People bound with chains of sin and demonic oppression.
....People who are frustrated and hopeless

Remember, No one can heal but God. "God is Healer" The same God who declared Himself to His people, Israel, as their healer, saying...." "I am the Lord that healeth thee..." (Exodus 15:26), is the same all powerful God who will heal all who come to Him in faith today. Through the word of God, you hold in your hands the potential for divine miracles. Receive your miracle of healing today, and go and help someone else receive tomorrow! Jesus Christ the anointed one will be with you, and he will heal.

Quick Reference To Healing Scriptures
Exodus 15:26 * Isaiah 53 * Psalm 103 * 1 Peter 2:24 *
Matthew 8:16-17
Matthew 8: 16-17 * Matthew 9:1-38
Mark 1:29-34, 40-45
Mark 1:1-12
Mark 3:1-6
Mark 5:1-20, 21-43
Mark 7:31-37
Mark 8:22-26
Mark 9:14-29
Luke 4:38-44
Luke 5:12-26
Luke 6:1-11
Luke 6:17-19
Luke 7:1-17
Luke 8:26-39
Luke 8:40-56

Chapter 7
The God Who Heals You

One of the names God reveals Himself by is Jehovah-Rapha' (rah-phah): Which means to cure, mend, restore to health, soundness and wholeness, To make free from all sickness and diseases. To live a successful Christian life, we must begin with knowing God is. In Exodus, God reveals part of His nature and character. Knowing God in truth will affect our behavior. This will lead us into a more faithful and fruitful lifestyle. When we truly come to know God and realize who He is, we will act differently, our commitment and dedication to Him will be stronger, we will make different choices, we will think more seriously about what we say and do. Understand that, GOD IS! His name is, "I AM THAT I AM". Rest on this foundation and be grounded and established in Him. Receive God as the "LORD WHO HEALS YOU". To heal is His nature; His will is to make you whole. Rely upon Him-your victory, miracles, your God is a good God. He desires only His very best for you. In promising His continuing healing presence as our healer, God places two great conditions before us: (Exodus 15:26).

First, God asks us to heed Him. He wants us to listen for His voice, to have a hearing ear, so we will hear Him. God has always spoken to His people and he will speak to you today, even now. But you must develop and attitude of listening to His word through His anointed servants, and through direct revelation in your inner man. (Eph. 1:17- 18), God seeks a people who will listen for His voice and not hesitate to obey Him.

> "Then it shall come to pass, because you have listened to these judgments, and keep and do them, that the Lord your God will keep with you the covenant and the mercy which He swore to your fathers.
>
> And He will love you and bless you; He will also bless the fruit of your womb and the fruit of your land,

your grain and your new wine and your oil, the increase of your cattle and the offspring of your flock, in the land of which He swore to your fathers to give you. You shall be blessed above all peoples; there shall not be male or female barren among you or among your livestock. And the Lord will take away from you all sickness, and will afflict you with none of the terrible disease of Egypt which you have known, but will lay them all on those who hate you". (Deut. 7:12-15).

God asks us to do what is right in His sight. Practice integrity and honor. We must become doers and not just hearers of the word. God's goodness is abundantly promised to those who sow to the spirit.

ATONEMENT AND ABUNDANT LIFE

Surely He has borne our griefs, And carried our sorrows, Yet we esteemed Him stricken, Smitten by God and afflicted. But He was wounded for our transgressions, He was bruised for our iniquities; The chastisement for our peace was upon Him, And by His stripes we were healed. (Isaiah. 53:4-5).

Both Matthew 8:17 and 1 Peter 2:24, quoted from Isaiah 53:1-12, Eight centuries before Christ, Isaiah clearly saw and spoke of the death of Christ. (the crucifixion) and more importantly, he revealed the purpose of the cross.

ATONEMENT

Atonement—The reconciliation of God and man through the death of Jesus Christ, Reparation for an offense or injury. (Eph. 2:16, Col. 1:20, Rom. 5:10, 2 Corn. 5:19-20). To be our perfect High Priest, Jesus had to know our griefs by experience.

Recently, I read a story about two brothers, they were identical twins, both of them earned a living by driving taxi, one was married, the other unmarried, one day the married brother accidentally hit a man with his taxi and killed him, though it was an accident, he was charge with first degree man-slaughter, and was sentenced to a twenty-year prison term. The single brother decided that his brother needed to be with his family, so he went and visited his brother in prison, that day, he switched clothes with his brother, because they were identical twins, no one could tell them apart, so the guilty brother walked out a free man, the other brother took his place. This story is very close to what Jesus did for us, He took our place!

Jesus became your substitute, He took your place. He died the death that you deserved to die. He allowed himself to become sin to give you righteousness, He took on your sickness and disease, so you can be healed. He carried your griefs and sorrows to make you free, well and whole. In Christ' suffering and death, he bore more than our sins. The wages of sin is death, but he did not need to suffer as he did to atone for sin.

In this we see why he suffered. He suffered to bear our griefs and sorrows. He suffered for our peace and healing. Atonement for sin is our greatest need, yet, God sent his son to suffer and die for the whole man. He provided more than escape from judgment and hell burning with brimstone and fire, he made provision for a life of abundance. You have just as much right to prosper and be healed as you have the right to be saved. Divine prosperity and healing for every area of you life is a vitally equal part of salvation.

Divine healing is already included in the atoning work of Christ, His suffering and His cross. Healing for your mind, and body, healing for every part of your life. Your emotional life, your social life, and your financial life. Through the death and resurrection of Jesus Christ, God brought healing to your entire life. But neither is automatic. You must believe the word and accept the finished work of the cross. You must believe that he really bore your sicknesses and carried your infirmities away from you. You must believe the divine exchange, that he took your sickness and gave you his health.

You must believe the healer, Jesus Christ (the anointed one) lives inside of you. You can have no doubt concerning the word of God. Now it is up to you to cooperate with the Holy Spirit and partake in all that Jesus has provided for you. You can no longer be a spectator, you must become a participator. Lay hold to the provision and the promises of God by faith. A soul's eternal salvation or a person's temporal, and physical healing must be received by faith.

The Hebrew word for "grief and sorrows" most specifically means physical afflictions, not excluding emotional or any other.

Many are the afflictions of the righteous, But the Lord delivers him out of them all. (Psalm 34:19)

"Many evils confront the (consistently) righteous, but the Lord delivers him out of them all". (AMP)

"He sent His word and healed them, And delivered them from their destructions". (Ps. 107:20)

Maybe you have willfully violated some known boundaries and transgressed against God in some act of disobedience as each one of us has done in times past. Don't give up hope, God is a good God, ready to forgive and heal you everywhere you hurt right now, In (Ps. 107, sickness is the punishment for transgression. To transgress is to willfully violate known boundaries of obedience. The punishment is not so much a direct action of God's will as it is an indirect result of our having violated the blessings within the set boundaries of His will, and thus, having exposed ourselves to the judgments outside it. However, deliverance will come with genuine repentance. If you truly repent and call upon the name of the Lord, the Lord will deliver you. But, this is not God's best for his children, God wants us to walk in complete and total victory in every area of our lives every day, but, if you should find yourself in a fallen or compromised position, call upon the name of the Lord, the Lord will surely send help to you. "For the scripture says, whoever believes on Him will not be put to shame. For there is no distinction between Jew and Greek, for the same Lord over all is rich to all our lives". Difficulty or severe sickness may arrest us from our careless spiritual backsliding. But in this verse it is implied that when the Lord is sought with a contrite (a truly repentant) heart, God will deliver you and reverse the calamity and heal you spiritually and physically. There is no sickness that God cannot heal when his word is believed and acted upon. The lord will hear your cry and when he does, he will heal you with his word.

"And this is the confidence (the assurance, the privilege of boldness) which we have in him; [We are sure] that if we ask anything (make any request) according to His will (in agreement with His own plan), He listens to and hears us; And if (since) we (positively) know that He listens to us in whatever we ask, we also know (with settled and absolute knowledge) that we have (granted us as our present possession) the request made of Him". (John 5:14-15 AMP).

FAITH ALWAYS DEMANDS MORE THAN YOU CAN DO

I cannot tell you why instant manifestation is not always the case, sometimes healing is a process. However, no matter how long it seems you have to wait it is only for a season, it's only temporary, this too shall pass!

"Now it happened as He went to Jerusalem that He passed through the midst of Samaria and Galilee. Then as He entered a certain village, there met Him ten men who were lepers, who stood afar off. And they lifted up their voices and said, "Jesus, Master, have mercy on us" So when He saw them, He said to them, "Go, show yourselves to the priest. And so it was that as they went they were healed". (Luke 17:11-14)

Sometimes we just have to wait. However, as you go, as you move in the spirit of God, obeying His word, doing His will, ministering healing to others, you will be healed. And as we wait, God gives us the grace to wait patiently and endure any hardship attached that we may face while we wait. You wait with patient because you have confidence, you know that God heard your prayer because you have asked according to his will (in line with His word) therefore you know you have what you have asked for.

When you ask God to heal you, see it or not, by faith you know that you are healed.

> "But those who wait for the Lord (who expect, look for, and hope in Him) shall change and renew their strength and power, they shall lift their wings and mount up (close to God) as eagles (mount up to the sun), they shall run and not weary, they shall walk and not faint or become tired". (Isaiah 40:31 AMP)

With hope in place, your faith will not waiver.

> "Now faith is the substance of things hoped for, the evidence of things not seen; (Hebrews 11:1) Now faith is the assurance (the confirmation, the title deed) of the things [we] hope for, being the proof of things [we] do not see and the conviction of their reality [faith] perceiving as real fact what is not revealed to the senses". (Hebrews 11:1 AMP).

I've seen a few instant manifestations in my time. Once we were in a healing explosion in Atlanta Georgia, there was a woman sitting about seven rows from me, she was sitting inside the row so I couldn't see her feet, but the Lord said to tell her to start walking and he would make the devil release it that night. I did not know this woman, so I did not understand what the Lord meant, but I obeyed. When the woman came out into the isle, to my surprise she had a cast on one foot up to the knees, I found out later that she had broken her foot three days prior to the meeting. I told her, "the Lord said if you will start walking he will make the devil release it tonight". In the beginning, she had a hard time trying to walk with two people helping her, but she just kept truing, after a while it got a little easier, she kept walking, and it kept getting easier, soon she didn't need any help, she started walking faster and faster, then she started to run and shout. That woman went home that night, had the cast cut off, and came to service the next morning wearing high heel shoes, healed by the power of God!

In April of 2004, God gave us a miracle that surpasses my imagination, (blew my mind). On this particular day, three of my sons and some of their friends were visiting. They along with my husband and my eighteen months old grandson were all hanging out in the kitchen. It was a cold winter day, so my husband had the oven on to help increase the heat, for a short moment, my husband turned his back on the oven, like all curious children, my grandson reached into the oven and grabbed the red element, I was in the bedroom resting, but when my grandson screamed,

I knew he had touched that oven, some how, I just knew, it was a scream from hell, I jumped up and ran to the kitchen, my husband had the baby in his arms, the baby was screaming, my husband was crying, the baby's dad was shouting, call 911, take him to the hospital, I could smell the burning flesh, I tried to stay calm, I kept saying to my husband, "give me the baby" but he was holding onto him as if for life, finally I had to pry the baby out of his arms, when I looked inside the baby's hand, I cringed at the sight, three of his fingers were burned to the bones, I felt faint, my hearted started to race, I could feel fear creeping into my mind, I didn't know what I was going to do, I picked up my anointing oil and headed for my prayer room, Two weeks before the incident, the Lord instructed me to meditate on (St. John 14:14), when I got in my prayer room, I quickly anointed his hand with oil, then, I said, "Lord this is your chance to prove your word", You said, "whatever I ask in your name, you will do it", "today, I'm asking Lord", then I said, "Lord, I've never done this, but I've heard that a person can call fire out of another person, today, I'm going to call the fire out of this baby's hand", when I opened my mouth to speak, the Lord said, "blow on it", when I blew on the baby's hand, the baby went fast to sleep, the baby slept for five hours without waking, while the baby was asleep, the Lord restored his hand back to Normal, with new skin and all, when the baby woke up, it was as if nothing ever happened, there was no trace or evidence that his hand was ever burned. To God be the glory!

GOD IS HEALER!

Then there are some cases where it seems waiting is our only option. Some years ago I suffered with an ulcer that had eaten a hole in my stomach about the size of a fifty-cent piece. I was in pain all the time, I couldn't keep any food down, every time I ate I threw up, there were times when it would hurt so bad that I would crawl in the bathroom, lay on the floor and curl up in a knot waiting for the pain to subside, I really didn't want my family to know how sick I was, I finally gave in and went to the doctor, after all of the examinations and testing, the doctor decided that surgery was necessary. As I drove home, pondering in my mind what the doctor had said, I was prompted to turn on the radio, when the radio came on I heard the voice of Kenneth Copeland talking about divine healing, I didn't know what that was, but I decided, if there is such a thing, I'm going to get me some divine healing. So I decided, instead of going back to the doctor, I'm going to get me some divine healing. I ordered the healing tapes that Kenneth Copeland was offering on his program. While I was waiting for the tapes to arrive, the doctor called to remind me how desperately I needed this surgery and how many ways I could die from this ulcer if I didn't have the surgery, but I told the doctor to give me a little while to think about it, meanwhile, I was getting sicker every day. After a few days the tapes arrived, from the very first day I begun to listen to the tapes, day and night (Joshua 1:8). When I went to work, I wore my ear plugs, when I was in my car, I had the cassette player on, when I was cleaning, cooking, etc. I was listening to the tapes. (IS. 53:4-5, St. Matthew 8:16-17, 1 Peter 2:24, PS. 107:20, PS. 103:1-6, St. Luke 5:12-26, St. Mark 9:24-29, St. Mark 5:21-42).

When I went to bed at night, I turned the tape player on, if I woke up during the night, I restarted the tape. The more I listened and confessed the word it seemed as if I was getting worse, but I held fast to my confession of faith. I stood on the word of God. I would speak to my body as if it were another person, I would tell my body, "no matter how you feel, no matter how much you hurt, the word of God says; "by the stripes of Jesus, "We Were Healed" and you will obey the word of God and be healed". I continued to listen and confess the word for eighteen months.

<u>Joshua !:8,</u> says, "Meditate in the word, day and night", this word meditate means more than just thinking about it or pondering it in your mind. Meditate….denotes an active recitation, a re-speaking of God's word and what is in line (agreement) with his word, thus they shall not depart from your mouth, Keep and guard your heart with all vigilance and above all that you guard, for out of it flow the springs of life. (Proverbs 4:23)

Keep your heart, value and protect your mind, don't let anything that is not nutritional to your spiritual health enter in through your eyes or ears. Protect your emotions, and will. (Proverbs 2:24-27) Your mouth, lips, eyes, and feet are physical symbols for communication, attention, and behavior.

You must be extra careful what you watch, hear (listen to) and say. The eyes and ears are the gateway to your soul; your mouth is what brings forth what is deposited in your heart. (Matt. 12:33-37) whatever is in your heart is what your mouth will speak; as you meditate in God's word day and night, the word is being deposited in your heart, (St. Luke 8:11), your mind is being renewed (changed) (transformed) by the word of God.

One morning I got up and went to the cabinet and reached for my pills, just as my hand touched the pill bottle, I heard a voice spoke to me, saying, "you don't need that, you're healed", I responded, "healed", you see this pain in my stomach"? (My stomach was hurting so bad), I said, "I don't call this healed", the voice spoke again, "you are healed", suddenly, it was like a light came on in my mind, my heart was filled with the truth of God's word, yes, I am healed, like a bolt the power of God hit me in my stomach and spread over my body like a warm blanket, when it subsided the pain was gone! "By his stripes we were healed", until this day I am healed from that ulcer. Praise God Forever and ever!

Whatever you're going through right now is nothing compared to what God is taking you to. God is working in you a greater weight of glory to be revealed in due season.

Chapter 8
GOOD CHEESE

A few months ago, I found myself being bombarded with difficulties on every hand. I call it, "The Big Mac Truck Syndrome" it was as though I was being hit from every side all at once. I was feeling very sorry for myself, I sunk to the lowest level of self pity, I found myself asking the usual questions, why me Lord? Why is it so hard? Why is everything going wrong? Etc. The Lord let me complain and mourn for a while without so much as a grunt, when I finally got quiet enough for him to speak to me, He said, "cheese will never be cheese until it go through the process, and good cheese take more processing, because good cheese is not made to be served at the commoner's table, it's made to be served at the King's table, so cheer-up, you'll be cheese in a minute".

Let's face it, if you're going somewhere, you're going to have to go through something to get there. If you're headed for the Palace, you will go through the pit and the Prison. Before you reach the next level, there is some pruning that has to be done, there is some cutting away of the dead branches, some cutting out of the rotten stuff that is needed. There is some stuff in you that cannot go to the next level, you can't fly with too much weight. The shape you're in will not fit into the next level, so God has to melt you down and pour you into a different mold, give you a new shape for your new level, the anointing does not come without pain. The oil cannot flow until the olive is crushed. There will be no new wine until the grapes are pressed, God cannot put new wine into old wineskins. don't accept your present situation as your permanent revelation, whatever you're going through, it's only for a season, a time of preparation, you're going through the process to get to your progress, without the process there will never be any progress.

You're going through the commotion to get to your promotion, so look beyond where you are right now, stop living in your present situation and start living in your future revelation, this is not the end, it's just the beginning, the best is yet to come.

> **"For I know the thought that I think toward you, says the Lord, thoughts of peace and not evil, to give you a future and a hope. Then you will call upon me and go and pray to Me, and I will listen to you. And you will seek me and find me, when you search for me with all your heart. (Jeremiah 29:10-13)**

When you're going through a process of some type, the wise thing to do is seek God, get your focus on the source of divine direction. Through- out scripture we find repeated references to God's people seeking after Him. Implied in these passages is a quest for God that includes a level of intensity beyond what might be termed ordinary prayer. The word "search" along with the phrase "with all your heart" suggest an earnestness that borders on desperation. When you find yourself fighting a terminal illness, and every doctor you've gone to, has given his final word, "there is nothing I can do" you're in a desperate situation, it's time to seek God, it's time to search for the source of divine healing. The word "search" (Hebrew darash) suggests a "following after" or close pursuit of a desired objective; it also implies diligence in the searching process. King Solomon says,

> **"My son, give attention to my words, incline your ear to my sayings. Do not let them depart from your eyes. Keep them in the midst of your heart. For they are life to those who find them. And health to all their flesh". (Proverbs 4:20-23).**

When dealing with an adverse situation, such as, sickness, you must maintain your focus. I repeat you must keep your focus on the word of God, on God's promises concerning your life and your particular situation. Search the scriptures and find out how God feels about sickness and disease, find out that it is God's will for you to be well and whole, don't accept any report that tells you that God has put this sickness on you to teach you something, don't accept any report that says, "you just have to live with it" the devil is a liar. Refuse to accept the devil's lies. Stand on the word of God, speak the word of God, don't say anything but what the word says, hold on to the confession of your faith, God's word is the solution to your problem, don't speak the problem, speak the solution, "with the stripes that wounded him, "We Were Healed".

> **(Psalm 103:1-5) Bless the Lord, O my soul, and all that is within me, bless His Holy name! Bless the Lord, O my soul, and forget not all His benefits; Who forgives all your iniquities, who heals all your diseases, who redeems your life from destruction, who**

> crowns you with lovingkindness and tender mercies,
> who satisfies your mouth with good things, that your
> youth is renewed like the eagle's.

This is a definite promise of bodily healing based upon the character of Yehweh as the healer, it is clear that the dimension of healing promised here is specifically to include physical wholeness. The text reinforces the healing covenant, since the Hebrew word tachawloo (disease) is from the same root (chawiah) as the word for "disease" in Ex. 15:26, (makhaleh), further, the words for "heal" are the same in both passages (Hebrew- rapha), the distinct meaning involving the idea of mending or curing.

The two texts form a strong bond (Deut. 19:15; 2Corn. 13:1). These two verses bear witness from the OT that the Lord not only forgives iniquities, He heals our diseases. If under former covenant bodily healing was pointedly included with the Father's many other benefits, we can rejoice and rest in faith. The new Covenant "glory" exceeds everything of the old (2 Corn. 3:7-11), and we can be certain that God, in Christ, has made a complete provision for the well-being of our total person. Keep your heart; Value and protect your mind, emotions and will.

> "And do not be conformed to world, but be transformed by the renewing of your mind, that you may prove what is that good and acceptable and perfect will of God". (Romans 12:2).

GOING THROUGH THE PROCESS

> "This Book of the Law shall not depart from your mouth, but you shall meditate in it day and night that you may observe to do according to all that is written, For then you will make your way prosperous, and then you will have good success." (Joshua 1:8)

Don't fight against your process, work with it, and cooperate with god As he takes you through it. When a woman goes into labor, if she fight against the labor, the process of birth is harder, than it would be if she just work with it and cooperate with the attending medical staff. Look beyond the pain to the joy of deliverance that is set before you. Jesus was able to endure the cross because of the joy that was set before Him.

(Hebrews 12:2). Take the word God and visualize where you're going. If trial seem unbearable, know that God will not allow any temptation to come upon you that you are not able to bear, and at the right time he will reveal the way of escape. (1Corn: 10:13) God will get you out, God will deliver you. It's working for your Good, the gain will be greater than the pain. The glory will be Greater than your sad story, god is making good cheese out of you!

The Hebrew writer encourages steadfast faith by reviewing the victorious experiences of faith heroes, by providing not a definition, but a description of working faith. Faith is established conviction concerning things not seen and settled expectation of future rewards. We must have faith if we expect to receive anything from God, healing or otherwise.

"But without faith it is impossible to please God".(Hebrews 11:6) It is impossible to receive faith without the word.(Rom. 10:17)

Nothing pleases God like a steadfast faith in all that he is and promises to do. Faith believes what God says and acts in line with his word. Faith allows the believer to enter the rest which God has called us. Faith acknowledges the complete work of salvation while faithfully obeying every instruction from God.

The Greek word for substance literally means "a standing under," and was used in the sense of "of title deed". The main idea is that of standing under the claim to the property or item to support it's validity. Thus' faith is the title deed of things hoped for. Therefore it must be emphasized that assurance rest on God's promises.

The heroes of the old testament did not obtain a good report because of their great achievements, special holiness, or non-active acceptance of the Devine promises of God, but by an active certitude expressed in obedience, persistence, and sacrifice.

But let him ask in faith' with no doubting, for he who doubts is like a wave of the sea driven and tossed by the wind. For let not that man suppose that he will receive anything from the lord, he is a double minded man, unstable in all his ways. (James 1:6-8). A double minded man is a person drawn in two opposite directions, he is trying to hold on to faith in one hand and struggling with doubt in the other, being tossed to -and-fro. One day he believes that he is healed, the next day, he says he is sick, the next day he is not sure {double-minded}. His allegiance is divided and because of his lack of sincerity he vacillates between belief and unbelief, sometimes thinking that god will help him and at other times giving up all hope in Him. Such a person is unstable in all his ways, not only in his prayer life. The lack of consistency in his exercise of faith betrays his general character. Therefore, {inheriting} the promise is the outcome of faith and depends {entirely} on faith, in order that it might be given as an act of grace (unmerited favor), to make it stable and valid and guaranteed to all his descendants-not only to the devoted ones and keepers of the law, but also to those who share the faith of Abraham, who is the father of us all.

As it is written, I have made you the father of many nations, {He was appointed our father} in the sight of God in whom he believed, who gives life to the dead and speaks of nonexistent things that {He has foretold and promised} as if they {already} existed.(Gen. 17:5).

One of the important teachings of the Bible is concerning the words we speak. "Abram" means "High Father ' or "Patriarch" "Abraham means "Father of a multitude." Thus, God was arranging that every time Abraham heard or spoke his own name, he would be reminded of God's promise to him.

God has made you some promises, and besides, God's written word is His promise to you. Let God's word, which designated His will and promise for your life, become as fixed in your mind and as governing of your speech as God's changing Abraham's name was in shaping his concept of himself. Do not "name" yourself any less than God does.

Remember that Abraham believed God, against all odds he believed God, he spoke the promises of God until they were manifested, he didn't give up on God. He made some mistakes, but he didn't stop believing God. You may make some mistakes, you may break a few rules before the word come to pass in your life, but even when it looks hopeless, don't give up, the promises are still true, and God's word will come to pass. Just speak what God speaks in His word. Watch your mouth, what you say is what you get.

> "For as the rain comes down, and the snow from heaven; and do not return there, But water the earth, and make it bring forth and bud, that it may give seed to the sewer' and bread to the eater, so shall my word be that goes forth from my mouth; it shall not return to Me void, but, it shall accomplish what I please, and it shall prosper in the thing for which I sent it". (IS. 55:10-11). "So shall My word be that goes forth out of My mouth; it shall not return to Me void [without producing any effect, useless], but it shall accomplish that which I please and purpose, and it shall prosper in the thing for which I sent it. (IS. 55:11 AMP).

God's word can never be fruitless or barren. God's promises and plans (words) are as sure of fulfillment as the fact that it rains and snow. God's word, spoken in faith, spoken consistently and persistently will always have a positive effect, God's word will never prove useless, but will always accomplish it's assignment.

> (Mark 11:12-14)... Now the next day, when they had come out from Bethany, He was hungry. And seeing from afar a fig tree having leaves, he went to see if perhaps He would find something on it. When He came to it, He found nothing but leaves, for it was not the season for figs. In response Jesus said to it, "Let no one eat fruit from you ever again, " And His disciples heard it. (verses 20- 24...Now in the morning, as they saw the fig tree dried up from the roots. And Peter, remembering, said to Him, 'Rabbi, look! The fig tree which you cursed has withered away." So Jesus answered and said, " Have faith in God. For

assuredly, I say to you, whoever says to the Mountain, " Be removed and cast into the sea, 'and does not doubt in his heart, but believes that those things he says will be done, he will have whatever he says. Therefore I say to you, whatever things you ask when you pray, believe that you receive them, and you will have them.

MOUNTAINS OBEY YOUR FAITH!

There is a positive lesson to be learned from the cursing of the fig tree. The power of believing prayer. A mountain is symbolic of an obstacle, hindrance, or insurmountable problem. You do not have to become a mountain climber, your faith is a mountain mover. Faith is the key that releases the resources of heaven into our situation.

DON' TRY TO CLIMB YOUR MOUNTAIN SPEAK TO IT!!!!!

"And Jesus, replying, said to the, Have faith in God [constantly]. Truly I tell you, whoever says to this mountain, be lifted up and thrown into the sea! And does not doubt at all in his heart but believes that what <u>he says</u> will take place, it <u>will</u> be <u>done</u> for him". (St. Mark 11:22-23 AMP).

"Lord, who has believed our report? So then, faith cometh by hearing, and hearing by the word of God". (Romans 10:17).

"This book of the law shall not depart from your mouth, but you shall meditate in it day and night, that you may observe to do according to all that is written in it. For then you shall make your way prosperous, and then you will have good success". (Joshua 1:8).

You may find these same scriptures many other times in this book, but I feel the need to emphasize them in this place. It really concerns me, that it seems that we receive very little of the positive things we say. There is no problem getting the negative things we speak to come to pass. Maybe, it's because we are more consistent in speaking the negative than we are the positive. Before we can speak from a heart of faith, we must have faith in our hearts, our hearts must be so filled with faith until there is no room for doubt. If faith comes by hearing and hearing by the word of God, then we must hear the word. We must hear the word until our minds are change and conformed to the word. It's not Man's faith in God that removes mountains, it's God faith in man. We must have "God's faith" "the faith of God in our hearts". Our hearts has to be impregnated with the Word of God, the word must expand in our hearts like a baby grows in a mother's womb, it has to expand and grow to the point where we can no longer contain it on the inside, then we can give birth to faith through the words which we speak.

I do not know what mountains you're facing today. Maybe it's a mountain of financial problems, a mountain of stress, oppression, depression, marital problems, your children may be giving birth out of wedlock, or they may be hooked on drugs, practicing prostitution, or they may be in prison or worse. Maybe you've received a bad report from a doctor and now you're battling some incurable disease, what are you going to do?

You're not going to panic, you're going to pick up your courage, pick up your hope, pick up the word of God, and meditate in it day and night, you're going to study the word, you're going to hear the word, you're going to speak the word until you see nothing but the word. You're going to take every thought into captivity. Your mountains are subject to you in the name of Jesus.

Sometimes it seem like mountains come up out of no where for no apparent reason, unexpected situations, but don't let them scare you, your "mountain like" obstacles DO NOT have authority over you! They cannot stop the will of God from being performed in your life! It looks BIG and immovable! It seems like quite a stumbling block! Look at it, square in the eye, DEMAND it, COMMAND it to MOVE! How dare it stand in God's way, which is in you! It's not hindering you, but God's plan in you! It cannot stop the move of God in YOU!

You've prayed about the mountain, you've talked about the mountain, you've cried about the mountain, you've told others about the mountain, you've looked at it, you've tried to walk around it, but its too big, you've tried climbing it, but its too high. You are not call to pray, cry or talk about the mountain, you're not called to climb the mountain, when you try to climb the mountain you're trying to overcome or conquer it in your own physical strength or natural abilities.

You cannot overcome or conquer spiritual matters with natural or physical abilities. Sickness, disease, infirmities, poverty, oppression, stress, depression, marital problems, drugs, addictions. The root cause of all these are spiritual, ruled and manifested by the spiritual forces of darkness.

> **"My son, give attention to my words, incline your ear to my sayings. Do not let them depart from your eyes; Keep them in the midst of your heart; For they are life to those who find them, and health to all your flesh". (Proverbs 4:20-22).**

You're always tempted to look at the mountain but, if you keep the word of God before your eyes, you can't see the mountain. The word of God will cause your mountain to become insignificant, like taking off on a plane. When you board a plane, and it's ready for take off, it heads down the runway, as long the plane is on the ground, no matter how fast it's moving, you can still see the objects on the ground, cars, building, people, etc. but, when the plane lifts and begins to climb, the objects on the ground becomes less and less visible, the plane climbs higher and higher, the objects on the ground becomes smaller, (less visible) the plane climbs higher until it gets caught up in the clouds, the plane Is so high above the earth until nothing on the earth can be seen, everything is now invisible and insignificant.

When you board the plane of God's word, as you meditate in the word day and night, pondering the word, speaking the word, regurgitating the word, like a cow does its food, until you have gotten every bit of value out of it, your plane will take off and head down the runway of faith, if you are consistent and persistent, your faith plane will begin to lift your mind, your hope and your expectation, but you must stay on the plane.

You're bound to hit a few bumps, bad weather, turbulence, but stay on the plane. If you're on Delta Airlines, just because you hit a few bumps, or the plane has a few problems, even if there is a threat of crashing, you don't jump off the plane, you don't abort, you do what you have to do but you stay on the plane, you stick with it, even if the plane goes down you stick with it. A Delta may go down, heaven and earth may pass away, but the word will stand forever.

"Therefore humble yourselves under the mighty hand of God, that, He may exalt you in due time. Casting all your care upon Him, for He cares for you". (1Pet. 5:6-7)

Consent and submit to God's word, keep the word before your eyes, your eyes and ears are the gateway to your soul. God's word is health and healing to all your flesh. You must be careful what you allow to get into your heart through your eyes and ears. You must protect your heart at all cost, for out of your heart flows the springs of life. Put away from you false and dishonest speech, and willful and contrary talk; don't say anything that is not in line with the word of God, if the word don't say it, don't you say it! Death and life are in the power of the tongue.

(Prov. 18:21) For by your words you will be justified and acquitted, and by your words you will be condemned and sentenced. (Matt. 12:37). As you continue, the plane of the word will soon begin to lift you up, as you go higher, drawing nearer to God, renewing your mind, filling your heart with the word of faith, your mountain will become less and less visible, soon your mountain will become invisible and very insignificant. You cannot overcome or conquer spiritual matters with natural or physical abilities. Sickness, Disease, Infirmities, Poverty, Oppression, Stress, Depression, Marital problems, Drugs, Addictions, the root cause of all these are spiritual, ruled and manifested by the spiritual forces of darkness. There are no natural solutions for these, yes, you may find temporary relief, or find a way to mask the symptoms, but to conquer or dispel them you must deal with them for what they are, "Spiritual Affairs". You cannot expect to win when you engage in Spiritual Warfare with natural, carnal or physical weapons.

> (2 Corinthians 10:4-5) "For the weapons of our warfare are not carnal, but mighty in God for pulling down strongholds, casting down arguments and every high thing that exalts itself against the knowledge of God, bringing every thought into captivity to obedience of Christ." and blood], but they are might before God for the overthrow and destruction of strongholds, [Inasmuch as we] refute arguments and theories and reasonings and every proud and lofty thing that sets itself up against the [true] knowledge of God; and we lead every thought and purpose away captive into the obedience of Christ [the messiah], the anointed one". (AMP)

> "The world is unprincipled. It's a dog-eat-dog out there! The world doesn't fight fair. But we don't live or fight our battles that way…..never have and never will. The tools of our trade aren't for marketing or manipulation, but they are for demolishing that entire massively corrupt culture. We use our powerful God tools for smashing warped philosophies, tearing down barriers erected against the truth of God, fitting every loose thought and emotion and impulse into the structure of life shaped by Christ. Our tools are ready at hand for clearing the ground of every obstruction and building lives of obedience into maturity. (The Message Bible),

Our warfare is not against flesh and blood (Ephesians 6:12), therefore carnal [weak-worldly] weapons will not do. We need weapons that are God-Empowered, [Mighty in God]. The purpose is for pulling down [demolishing] strongholds (anything opposing God's will). Here Paul refers specifically to warfare in the mind, against arrogant, rebellious ideas and attitudes (which he terms, arguments) and against every high thing (pride) opposed to the true knowledge of God. The aim is to bring every disobedient thought into obedience to Christ. To make every thought, every argument, every word, every theory, shut up, listen and surrender to what Christ (the word of God has to say).

> (Mark 4:24-25 KJV) Then He said to them, "Take heed what you hear, with the same measure you use, it will be measured to you, and to you who hear, more will be given. For whoever has to him more will be given; but whoever does not have, even what he has will be taken away."

> (Mark 4:24-25 AMP) And He said, "Be careful what you are hearing. The measure [of thought and study] you give [to the truth you hear] will be the measure [of virtue and knowledge] that comes back to you…..and more [besides] will be given to you who hear."

Jesus appeals for spiritual perception. Those who receive and assimilate truth will have their capacity for understanding enlarged and their knowledge increased. It is very important what you listen to and put thought into. (Faith comes by hearing, and hearing, by the word of God. Romans 10:17).

When you receive and unfavorable report from a doctor, or any other voice of authority, because he is the voice of authority, and you respect him as being an expert in this field, you really have to be careful as to how you measure his words, and how much thought you put into them. Words are not only powerful, but they are spiritual. Words are used to paint pictures in our minds and spirits [heart]. Spoken words are like seed sown into the ground, if they are given the chance to germinate and grow up they will bring forth a harvest after their own kind. (Negative or positive). To stop the progress or growth of negative words, you need a weapon of greater potential or more powerful than the words of the medical authority. God's word must become your final authority; God's word must settle every issue. You cannot waiver, (James 1:2-8).

You're not denying the facts, you're just denying the devil parking rights. Your body is the temple of the Holy Ghost, the temple of God, and the devil has no right to park on God's property. If you enter someone's property that has a no trespassing sign posted, if you are caught trespassing by the owner, the owner has a right to do what he wants with you, usually he will let the law handle it, the same with you, let the law handle it. When the devil attack your body or mind with some type of sickness, disease or infirmity, he's trespassing on God's property.

> **(Hebrew 4:12 NKV) For the Word of God is living and powerful, and sharper than any two-edged sword, piercing even to the division of soul and spirit, and of joints and marrow, and is a discerner of the thoughts and intent of the heart.**
>
> (Hebrews 4:12 AMP) For the word that God speaks is alive and full of power [making it active, operative, energizing and effective] it is sharper than any two-edged sword, penetrating to the dividing line of the "breath of life (soul) and [the immortal] spirit, and of joints and marrow [of the deepest parts of our nature], exposing and sifting and analyzing and judging the very thoughts and purpose of the heart" The word of God is the seed. (St. Luke 8:11).

(St. Mark 4:30-32) Then He said, "To what shall we liken the Kingdom of God? Or with what parable shall we picture it? It is like a mustard seed, which, when it is sown on the ground, is smaller than all the seeds on the earth, but when it is sown, it grows up and becomes greater than all herbs, and shoots out large branches, so that the birds of the air may rest under its shade.

(Ephesians 6:12) "For we do not wrestle against flesh and blood, but against principalities, and powers, against the rulers of the darkness of this age, against spiritual wickedness in the heavenly places".

Have faith, believe, DON'T DOUBT....and TELL THE MOUNTAIN TO MOVE! Keep going your way, making progress....resist the obstacle, embrace the God-life, really embrace it, and nothing will be too much for you. Every obstacle, every hindrance, every mountain WILL become invisible, it can never stand against God's purpose to be accomplished. Stand in your authority and speak God's word of life into and at your "mountain-like" obstacles. They are standing in God's way, not yours! Watch God take it down to a size smaller than His word!

SPEAK TO THE MOUNTAIN....it will both listen and obey your faith!!!!!

SAVED BY GOD'S HAND

Jesus is Lord over every mountain, symbolic or real. Many years ago, we lived in Rochester, N.Y., my husband and I along with our three children. The Lord blessed us with very good jobs, we made very, very, good money, we had a very nice five bedroom home, life was pretty good, we were in a good church, the shopping malls and almost everything was at our finger tips, not like in the country where you have to drive forty or fifty miles to find a mall, or drive ten or fifteen miles just to buy some groceries, there, all I had to do was walk across the street to shop for groceries. I had no complaints I was happy with our lives. I worked during the day, while my husband watched the children, my husband worked at night, this arrangement worked out very well for us, we didn't really know anyone there, so we took care of each other.

My husband's mother was a widow that raised four children on her own, along with two or three others raised as her own, and now she was practically raising six grand children. I understand more now of what she was dealing with. Don't get me wrong, I loved my mother-n-law and I would do anything I could for her, and I understood very well that I was married to her only son and her youngest child. Every Sunday morning she called, and during the conversation she never failed to remind him what a burden she was bearing in practically having to raise the children, and she needed help with the farm. Needless to say, my husband was ready to pack up, disrupt our lives and move back to the South to help his mother. Maybe I would've done the same thing had it been my mother, but moving back to the South was never my intention.

One day my husband came home and announced, "we're moving to South Carolina" "WHAT, ARE YOU OUT OF YOUR MIND?" I argued, I fussed, I cried for two weeks, but nothing I said made any difference, he wouldn't take no for an answer, and he wouldn't wait for winter to pass. It was in the middle of winter, snow was ankle deep, but we just had to leave now.

One very icy cold February day, he went out and rented a U-Haul, packed us up and we were on our way. We owned two cars, he pulled the U-haul behind his car, and I followed in mine. I thought I was totally crazy to let him talk me into this, but what was I suppose to do? I kept thinking, this is the worse day of my life, I got into the car with tears streaming down my face, I made up my mind that day, I will hate him for the rest of my life, I already hated where we were going so hating him shouldn't be a problem.

As we started out on this suicide mission, we ventured out on the interstate, cars were bumper to bumper, sliding, skidding off the road, across the road, every which way, I just knew he would say, "let's turn around and go back" this was no two-hour drive, but he didn't. Thinking that it would be better, he finally, gave me the signal to turn and go another way that would take us through the high mountains, it was worse but once on there is no way off for many miles, very determined we Kept going, creeping along like snails, it began to snow again, the highway was barely visible, by now, I have forgotten about hating him, all I'm doing now is praying, I just want to get there in one piece. I had the baby and my brother in the car with me, I was so afraid, I didn't know what to do, I can't turn around and go back. If you've ever traveled the mountains, you know how narrow and steep the road can be. Suddenly cars started slipping and sliding, bumping into each other, there were many accidents, but people were not waiting around for the patrol, they exchanged information and kept on creeping the best they could.

Suddenly, my car hit an ice pocket, it started sliding and spinning, the front of the car headed for the edge of the mountain, there are no shoulders, no side embankment, just steep narrow road on the top of a mountain. My car is going over the edge, the car is falling, it was as if time stopped, I'm thinking, "we're going to die and my husband will not know what happened to us" I forgot words to pray, I didn't remember how to pray, or what to pray. I looked up through the windshield and said, "God if you don't stop this car I'm done", suddenly, God did the impossible. A hand reached out of the side of the mountain and caught my car, the car stopped falling and came to rest in the hand of God. I sat there in shock, stunned out of my mind. I'm thinking, my car has fallen off the mountain and I can't see the bottom, if we hit the bottom, they will never find us, I looked in the back seat, thank God everyone is asleep. Finally my brother woke up, asking why have we stopped? As he attempted to pull up and look out of the window, the car cracked a little, I said, don't move, we've skidded off the road. He said looks more like we've flown off the mountain, what are we going to do? I thought, "good question?". Ok, God, "thank you for saving us", but what now? I heard, "flash your headlights off and on", this time the command was stronger, so I started flashing. I don't know exactly how long I flashed, but It was a long time, but I just kept flashing. I didn't understand the purpose, but I kept flashing. God is so amazing and so awesome, there is no comparison.

There was a truck driver somewhere on the highway, according to his estimate, about one hundred miles away. I can only repeat what he told us….. Somehow God drew his attention to the headlights bouncing off the trees and he recognized it as an S.O.S, he knew someone was in trouble, and he felt compelled to find them. He said he drove and drove, searching for us, the bad weather did not make it easy for him, it would have been very easy for him to have gone his own way, but he felt compelled. Finally when he got to the place where we were, all he could see was a car suspended in air, he could not see the hand that was holding us up. He said, "I begun to pray, lord, I've got to help those people, but you've got to help me", I don't know what to do. By the time he got finished praying, an idea came to him, set up flashers on the highway, by the time he got the flashers set up, another truck driver came along, on that truck was everything that they needed to get us back up to the highway. By some miracle they were able to join the two trucks together, they dropped two hundred and twenty feet (225) of chain down off that mountain, wrapped it around my car and pulled us back on to the highway. When my husband missed us off the highway, he turned around and came searching for us, he got to us just before they pulled us back up to the highway, to this day, we are still in shock. To God be the glory. You may look at the situation right now and it seems like all hope is gone, but trust God it is not impossible for God to fix, there is nothing too hard for God to do, if you will trust him.

I pray that someday I will meet these two men or a member of their families, I just want to say, "<u>THANK YOU</u>". I will be eternally grateful to God and the two men that helped me that night. To the two men who helped me that night. Maybe by some chance you will read this account of what happened that night, or maybe you shared this with a member of your family, or someone else. If you are someone that has heard this account by one of those men that helped, please contact me by phone or mail. You may not remember our names, but I know you will never forget that night. I pray that the God who heard my prayer and sent you to rescue me will hear this prayer, and give me a chance to thank you in person. Again, THANK YOU.

MOUNTAIN MOVING FAITH

Jesus' action in cursing the fig tree indicates a passion in prayer and Faith that we need to learn. When the disciples noticed, with total surprise that the tree had withered completely. Jesus responded with a precise command, "have faith in God", then commanding them to "speak to the mountains", he led them to prepare for situation in which they would find it necessary to take direct authority in the spiritual realm to impact things in the natural realm.

FAITH CONFESSIONS

In these verses Jesus gives us direct and practical instructions concerning our exercise of faith. "Persistent faith, confessions produces successful visible possession"

It must be "in God" The God kind of faith. Faith that speaks is first faith that seeks. God is the source and grounds of our faith and being. Faith only flows to Him because of the faithfulness that flows from Him. Faith is not a trick performed with our lips, but a spoken expression that springs from the conviction of our hearts. The idea that faith's confession is a "formula" for getting things from God is unscriptural. But the fact that the faith in our hearts is to be spoken, and thereby becomes active and effective toward specific results, is taught by the Lord Jesus. "Whatever things" apply this principle to every aspect of our lives. The only restrictions are (a) that our faith be "in God" our living Father and in line with His will and word; and (b) that we "believe" not doubting in our hearts, thus, "speaking to the mountain" is not a vain or superstitious exercise or indulgence of our human mind, instead becomes an applied release of God's creative word of promise. Our words are filled with power to "Move Mountains" only when they are a reality in our hearts, and our mind (soul) and spirit are in total agreement. (Matthew 18:19).

ABUNDANT LIFE

"The thief does not come except to steal, and to kill, and to destroy, I have come that they may have life, and that they may have it more abundantly. (St. John 10:10). Abundantly; superabundance, excessive, overflowing, surplus, over and above, more than enough, profuse, extraordinary, above the ordinary, more than sufficient.

> **"Beloved, I wish above all things, that thou mayest prosper and be in health, even as thy soul prospereth. (1John 2).**

God desires absolute Biblical abundance for His children. As you give your total self to God, God gives His total self to you. Bible based abundance and prosperity is the real possibility of health for your total being, (body, mind, emotions, and relationships), of your material needs being met. Above all, His prosperity brings peace, joy, spiritual fulfillment and eternal life. Stop to think about it, what else can you want?

Jesus said that, "He came to give life" not just ordinary existence, but Life in fullness, abundance and prosperity. On the other hand the enemy (Satan) comes only to steal, kill and destroy. The line is clearly drawn, on one side is God with goodness, life and "plenty" of all that is necessary for life, and on the other side is the enemy of our souls, who comes to rob us of God's blessings, to oppress our bodies through sickness, diseases, and accidents, and to destroy everything that we love and care about. Your first step toward experiencing full biblical prosperity is to believe that it is God's highest desire for you. The next step is to line up your highest desire with His. God wants you well and whole in every area of your life. He wants you to have His best, abundant life.

God's covenant to us is a covenant for abundant life. From the very beginning of time, scripture shows us that God wanted us to be happy and prosperous. In Genesis, we are told that God made everything and declared it to be good. Then he gave this beautiful, bountiful, plentiful earth to Adam; Adam was given dominion over all of it. (Genesis 1:28). God's plan from the beginning was for man to be enriched and to have a prosperous, abundant life, Jesus declares His intention to recover and restore to man what was the Father's intent and to break and block the devil's intent to hinder our receiving it.

Christ came to earth in defense of life. By His words and action He opposed anything, force, or person that might diminish it. Likewise, He calls us to do everything within our power to preserve and enhance the lives of those around us. In addition to evangelizing, we are to work to reduce poverty, disease, hunger, injustice and ignorance.

Beyond His defense of life, however, Jesus also came to deliver from death and to introduce abundant living. By His death and resurrection, Christ has opened a new dimension of life for all mankind, that "all things become new" (2 Corn. 5:17). (NEW) Kainos (Kahee-noss). Unused, fresh, novel, meaning, new in form or quality, rather than new in reference to time. Christ death and resurrection for us, and our identification with Him by faith, make existence as a new creation possible for anyone that will believe and accept Him. Our relationship with Christ affects every aspect of our life.

Chapter 9
HE TOUCHED ME

There are some things that happens in our lives that is so devastating that its very difficult to share with anyone, but giving God glory for what He has done is far more valuable than a little discomfort or embarrassment we may experience. What I am about to share with you is one of those things. Its taken me this long to put it into words. I cannot give you medical documentation, because, first, the records were sealed, then later destroyed. The attending physician has retired, nevertheless, every word I am about to share with you is true. I know it will sound like something out of the dark ages or a horror movie. I share this for one reason and one reason only, that I might bring glory to God.

Thinking back on that year cause tears to flow from my eyes, its always fresh in my mind like it happened yesterday. New years night of 1977, I had a strange dream that disturbed me a lot. I didn't know what to make of it, but it made me very uneasy.

I dreamt, that I was cleaning my house when I heard a knock on the door, when I went to answer the door, I saw a woman and two men Standing there, but I realized that I didn't want them in my house because they had a reputation for dealing in witchcraft, so I stood between them and the door, talking, but not inviting them in. The lady said to me, "we know you have that baby in there, but you're going to need help", she then handed me some money and said, "take this and get some help for your self," I said to her, "I don't have a baby here, " but she insisted that I did. After they left, I stepped out of my back door, there was a dead alligator on the ground with its throat slit opened, an opossum had crawled into its throat and died. When I woke up I was frightened and confused. I didn't tell anyone about the dream, I just pondered it in my mind, but it wouldn't leave me.

We Were Healed

In March, I started feeing really bad all the time, my energy was depleted all the time, I could barely make it through the day, I was so weak, and my skin started turning dark. Around that time, I started having this recurring dream. At that time I lived in a mobile home, in the kitchen I had a built in wall oven. In my dreams, I would go into the kitchen, turn on the oven to bake, but realized that there was something in the oven, when I opened the oven, hundreds of fishes would begin flipping out of the oven, it always frightened me no matter how many times I had the dream.

The last week in may I decided to go to the doctor, after the exam, the doctor told me I was about six weeks pregnant, due to my history, this is not good. I was sick everyday, some days I could not get out of bed, my feet and hands were swollen out of proportion, my head hurt all the time, I was just very miserable. I grew twice as fast as any normal pregnancy. There was something strange about my skin, my skin got darker & darker, it was like my skin was growing scales. I was almost afraid of myself. I was so big, I no longer walked, I waddled, by the time I was four month along. I couldn't go anywhere but to the doctor. In October I went into labor, the doctor put me in the hospital for a few days and stopped the labor. October and November were the worst. The dreams came more frequently, I got larger and darker, the scales were more apparent, the doctor says, "We just have to wait and see". People are now urging me to go and see someone that deal with tarot cards, etc.

They would say, "you need to go and see about yourself", you need help"! What am I to do? Lord, help me!

The third Sunday in November, my husband took the children with him to church, I decided to hobble up and clean the house and make a good dinner, and that I did, but I noticed that flies were everywhere, they gathered in the windows by the masses, they seem to be hanging off the ceiling, they were just everywhere. Where did all these flies come from? There were so many of them it became scary, it seemed that everything I touched that day a swarm of flies would overtake it. When I saw that my husband and the children were returning home from church, I hurried as fast as I could to get dinner on the table, but, as soon as I filled a plate and sat it on the table, the flies would cover it, I had to throw out all of the food. I thought that I would lose my mind that day, but God is merciful, and he is able to keep us even in the midst of the darkest storm. I don't know how but somehow God gave me the strength to get through the events of that terrible day. They tried to help me get rid of the flies, but it seemed hopeless, so my husband took the children out to get something to eat. Finally the flies left, just as mysteriously as they came, except for one (1), it seemed that this one fly just hung around buzzing all day, we just couldn't get rid of it, we tried everything, at night it would hang around in my bedroom, everywhere I went this fly was there, needless to say, this was quite unnerving.

That next Wednesday night around two o'clock, I got up and went in the bathroom, while I was in there something strange happened, I felt this extreme cold come over me, it was so cold, it felt like ice was running through my veins, I was shivering so hard, it felt like my joints were being pulled apart, somehow I made it back in the bed and got under the covers, my husband put more covers on me, but it got colder, I was so cold I thought I would pass out or die, this lasted about an hour, then I was normal again.

That next Sunday, I went into labor again, the doctor put me in the hospital again, but this time its for the remainder of the pregnancy. The doctors and nurses had the kind of look on their faces that they have when they have to break some kind of bad news to a patient. I knew I was in trouble, I just didn't know how serious it was. My room was right next to the nurses station so they could watch me, but I could also hear almost everything that was said, and most of what I heard was not good news. After they got me into bed, the doctor left the room and went out to the nurse's station, I could hear him on the phone talking to a specialist, he told him, "I need you now, I have a woman that's going to die if I don't do something right away". After he hung up and came back to my room. He began to engage in small talk, asking me how did I feel, etc. Finally, I asked him, what's wrong? He shook his head and said, "I don't know what to tell you, things don't look good, but we're going to get you some help".

Sunday, about four o'clock, the specialist arrived, he examined me, and told my doctor, "this is beyond me, call doctor A from NC." Dr. A came about eleven o'clock that night. Dr. A was just as puzzled as the others, by Monday evening, twenty two doctors had examined me, I will never forget the last Dr. that examined me, after the examination he pulled my doctor to the side and said, "she's a dead woman", later that evening they hooked me up to life support, they put a tube and a needle every place they could find to put one. Now comes the debate, shall we operate? If we operate she will not survive, if we don't operate, she's going to die. Meanwhile my mother was sitting by my bed, ever-so-often, she would anoint me with oil, and say, "in the name of Jesus". I thank God for my mother and her sticking with me, and her faith in God, she didn't give up, for six days she never left my side.

Several days has gone by with no improvement. That Thursday night, the doctor came in and said, "Rebecca, we're going to take you to surgery in the morning, we're going to do a C-section, the nurse will be in about five to prep you." I had already heard them say, if they operate I would die. For the first time since I was admitted to the hospital, I opened my mouth to speak. When I left home I took my Bible with me, but I had not read it until now. Oh yes, the fly is still here, even in the hospital, that fly kept flying by my room door. That night about eleven o'clock I asked my mom to hand me my Bible, I opened it to Ps. 91 and laid it on my chest, and said, "Lord, if I'm going to live through this surgery, let them take me in the morning, but if I'm not going to live and it's not time for me to die don't let them take me," and for the first time in six days I went to sleep. The next morning at five o'clock the nurse came in and prepped me for surgery, she said, we will be back for you at eight o'clock. Eight o'clock came, they didn't come, nine, ten, eleven o'clock I was still in my room, by this time for some reason unknown to us the hospital was in an uproar, we found out later that they came next door to my room and got the wrong lady and took her to surgery. (What a mighty God we serve). No surgery that day!! God is working it out.

That Saturday morning I took a turn for the worse, I was so sick until I didn't feel sick anymore, except for the labor pain, the pain is so bad, I've had four children already, so I know what labor pain feels like, this is something different, the pain is humanly unbearable, my body is giving out on me. If I don't get some relief I'm going to die. My mom is praying and anointing me with oil. Around two o'clock, something strange begins to happen. I heard a voice in my right ear that said, "6:30", I turned to my mother and said, "6:30 mama" what, she asked, I don't know, but "6:30".

Then my room started getting dark, it grew darker and darker, there was a sound like a storm caught in a jar, there were very dark clouds roaring, like the powers of hell had come to surface. It was very frightening, then for the first time, my mother jumped up and left the room. At that time, I began to cry out—-"Lord help me, please come and see about me". I kept crying out to the Lord, I remember hearing the familiar voice of a woman that said, "pray baby, you're calling on the right one".

I don't know what time it was when my spirit lifted from my body, but it was as if I was floating above my body. I could see the doctors and nurses working on my body, I could hear them screaming, "Code blue, Code blue, she's crashing, we're losing her". At that point my spirit left the room, I landed in the most beautiful garden that can be imagined, the flowers and trees were as though they were abundantly alive, more alive than any flower or tree that I had ever seen, they were bursting with robust, radiant colors and life. In the center of this garden was a Hugh tree, I remember thinking, this tree must've been here forever, somehow I knew if I could make it to this tree, everything would be alright. Seems like just thinking it was enough, no sooner than I thought it, I was at the tree, I bowed down at the tree, when I did that, my spirit returned to the room where they were still working on my body, I looked at my lifeless body, and the people working on it, I could tell that they were giving up hope. One of the doctors looked at his watch and said, "it's over, lets call it, death occurred at 6:26 pm". But I'm so glad that God has the last say, it's not over until God says it's over. I turned and looked over at the wall and saw Jesus walk right through the wall, He went straight to the bed where my body was lying there, so lifeless, so helpless, so hopeless, so alone, so mangled from being ravished by all the pain and so many hands poking at it, so many machines being hooked up to it, only Jesus could fix this.

Jesus stood at the bed, looked down at my body and smiled. He touched my forehead, and said, "go, tell my people to get ready and stay ready, for my coming is closer at hand than they think". Suddenly, my spirit, (my life) returned to my body, to everyone's surprise, I was alive! Precisely at 6:30 PM my deliverance came, my Michael was borne, a beautiful twelve pound baby boy, something is wrong, the nurse has the baby in her arms, but there seem to be another baby, something is still moving in my stomach, everyone is getting excited, they kept saying, "it looks like we are not finished, I believe we have another one", but how could this be? There was never any indication of a second baby. While they were trying to figure things out, shockingly, my fish dream came true right before our eyes. Suddenly, like a dam breaking loose, water came pouring (gushing) from my vagina, in the water were fishes, many, many fishes, they were flipping all over the floor, everyone was running and screaming, the doctor called for an orderly to bring a bucket, they were picking up fishes that came out of me as if someone had pulled in a net and dumped the fish on shore. I was so afraid, and ashamed, which is the reason why I have not been able to share this whole story with anyone before. I was laying there thinking, "I'm giving birth to fish, what in the world is this? While I was thinking about what was happening to me, someone said, "this is witchcraft, somebody got her good." Finally the fish stopped coming, they took them away in buckets, got me cleaned up and took me to my room. Later the doctor came in and talked to me, he didn't have any answers as to how the fish got inside me, why were they detected during examines, so he said that the records would be sealed.

In less than fifteen minutes my skin had returned to normal, I was completely delivered and made whole, I give praise to Jesus Christ our Lord, by whose stripes we were healed!! Not only did Jesus raise me from physical death that day, He also raised me from spiritual death. A few hours later the doctor came and sat down on the edge of my bed, took my hands in his and said, "I'm sorry, I can't explain why, but the baby didn't make it", I felt such pain in my heart, it hurt so much, I couldn't even cry, my beautiful baby, oh' how I wanted to hold him in my arms and make it ok, but he was gone, we named him Michael Kelyon, my husband and the children had a graveside burial service for him the next day, I could not attend because I was still in the hospital, a friend of ours took a picture, she gave it to me three months later, when I saw just how beautiful he was, I just could not understand how this could happen to an innocent baby.

Thank God for His love, grace and mercy. God protected me from experiencing the full hit of that horrific moment. Yes, I mourned my baby, but not until God knew I was ready. My heart was broken into so many pieces; if God had not protected me I wouldn't have been able to bear it, but God kept me at peace.

Chapter 10
Jesus Is Lord and God's Word Is the Final Authority

Each day I have the privilege to enjoy the company and friendship of my husband, I know without doubt, God's word is the final authority in every situation. I look at my husband and I thank God for His healing power. I know that there are still many people that does not believe in divine healing, nor do they believe in miracles, but I am a living miracle and I have the privilege of living with one.

It was not until I saw my husband stricken with a stroke that could have killed him or left him paralyzed for life, that I truly realized that Jesus Christ is Lord, and God's word is the final authority, sickness and disease is no match for the word of God. Above all, God wants us well and whole, and God is not please when we allow ourselves to fall prey to sickness and disease, something he already carried for us, something he already redeemed us from.

> "Surely he has borne our griefs, and carried our sorrows, yet we esteemed him stricken by God and afflicted. But he was wounded for our transgressions, he was bruised for our iniquities. The chastisement for our peace was upon him. And with his stripes we are healed." (IS. 53:4-5).

Surely he has borne' carried, means to take upon oneself or to carry as a burden. The gospel of Matthew declares,

> "When evening had come, they brought to him many who were demon possessed. And he cast out the spirits with a word, and healed all who were sick. That it might be fulfilled which was spoken by the prophet Isaiah, saying, "He himself took our infirmities, and bore our sickness." (Matthew 8:16-17).

The Amplified bible says,

"He himself took, [in order to carry away our weaknesses and infirmities and bore away our diseases]. "
"Beloved, I pray that you may prosper in every way and (that your body) may keep well even as (I know your soul keeps well and prospers". (3 John 2 AMP)

It was never God's intention for you to be sick or poor, in the beginning God created man and woman, strong, healthy, well and happy in fellowship with him. But Satan, the deceiver, caused Adam and Eve to disobey God and doubt His word. They sinned against God and yielded themselves to the authority of Satan. When Adam set aside the commandments that God had given him, and bowed his knees to Satan, he made Satan illegitimate ruler of this world, immediately things changed. The earth was cursed and everything in it. The kingdom of darkness came into power, death, sickness, disease, infirmities, poverty, oppression, and lack passed to all men. But we don't have to live under the curse any longer, Christ has redeemed us from the curse, having become the curse for us. (Gal. 3:13). Now that Jesus Christ has paid our debts and suffered our penalty, in our place, God has declared us free, through his blood we have redemption, and by His stripes we were healed. (Col. 1:14, 1 Peter 2:24).

Our salvation, our deliverance, our redemption, our freedom, from sin, sickness, diseases, poverty, and all the works of Satan have been accomplished by Jesus Christ. (St. John 19:28-30). "It is finished". It's a done deal. The battle has been fought, the enemy has been conquered and forced to surrender. (Col. 2:14-15).

The enemy has been wiped by our champion, Jesus Christ. Wiped-out, means to remove or cancel the power of sin, sickness, disease, poverty, lack and all other works of Satan.

(1 John 3:8) "For this purpose, Jesus, the son of God was manifested, (revealed) to destroy the works of the devil".

Jesus did what he came to do, He gave you back your original position. He raised you up and caused you to sit in heavenly places with Christ Jesus. And put all things under your feet. (Ephesians 1:22, 26). God, Through the events of the cross, stripped powers and principalities of their uncontested rule and authority over God's redeemed people who live under the lordship of Christ. "He made a public spectacle of them", does not mean that they have been gotten rid of, but their power and authority over the redeemed has been dis-armed.

"Even when we were dead in trespasses made us alive together with Christ, (by grace you have been saved), and raised us up together, and made us sit together in heavenly places in Christ Jesus". (Ephesians 2:5-6).

"And what is the exceeding greatness of His power toward us who believe according to the working of His mighty power. Which he worked in Christ when He raised Him from the dead and seated Him at His right hand in the heavenly places, far above all principalities and power and might and dominion and every name that is named, not only in this age but also in that which is to come, and he put all things under his feet, and gave him to be head over all things to the church which is his body, the fullness of Him who fill all in all". (Ephesians 1:19-23).

"Who Himself bore our sins in His own body on the tree, that we being dead to sins, might live unto righteousness, by who's stripes we were healed". (1 Peter 2:24).

Jesus is our example, here He is our redeemer, Jesus' death makes possible our response of death to sins (repentance) and life for God, (righteousness), which Peter describes. "by whose stripes you were healed", Peter is showing that personal wholeness, mental, physical, financial, social, and spiritual flows from salvation.

When we make Jesus our Lord, He becomes Lord and redeemer of every part of our life. Satan no longer have the right to afflict us with sickness and diseases, yet the people of God continue to get sick and die prematurely from all manner of diseases. If "we were healed", then why are we (the saints of God) so sick and feeble? Why are so many of the saints sitting in the doctor's waiting room every day, why are the hospitals filled with God's people?

For months, I had been praying, "Lord teach me how to apply your word concerning healing to my daily life, and help others receive healing through this word". My mind could not comprehend this mysterious word of God, but I knew it had something to do with the words of our mouths, the word and the power of the blood. I knew the word of God was the final authority in everything, as I continued to pray and seek God, He began to emphasize the importance of the words of our mouth, what we speak daily is what is manifested in our lives.

"Death and life are in the power of the tongue". (Proverbs 18:21).

The Lord begun to turn my attention to (Mark 11:22-26, Jos. 1:8, Ps.103:1-6, Proverbs 4:20-23, Romans 10:8-10, Jer. 33) and many others. I came to realize that healing and deliverance is in the word, and physical, emotional, mental, financial, and social healing is just as much a part of my salvation as missing hell and going to heaven. All must be received by faith, and they must be believed for and accepted daily. The question still remains. How do I get the healing that's in the word to manifest in my body? (Know the truth and the truth will make you free).

(Psalm 107:20, Romans 1:16, Proverbs 4:20). These verses intersperses at intervals the call to remember the importance of the truth being given. Keep your heart, guard your heart, value and protect your mind, emotions and will. Fill your heart with the word of God, make daily deposits of the word in you heart, to the point of impregnation. When a woman is trying to become pregnant, she does not always conceive on the first try, but if she is determined, she will keep going back to the source of the seed to receive the deposit, so it is with the word of God.

(The word of God is the seed. St. Luke 8:11) (So then, faith comes by hearing and hearing, by the word of God. (Rom: 10:17)

We must keep hearing and hearing the word, we must keep going back to the source of the seed for the deposit, we must deposit the seed of the word in our hearts, by hearing the word over and over again, until the word is conceived in our hearts as a baby is conceived in a mother's womb.

Even after a woman has conceived, she does not stop going to the Source, even so, she goes more freely, because her fears or doubts of becoming pregnant has been dispelled, and her desire for that which impregnated her is increased. So it is with the word of God, when faith is conceived in our hearts and begins to grow and show, we must continue going to the source of faith (the word of God). We must keep depositing the word of God in our hearts, so that we will have a continuous harvest. Don't allow anything else to enter your heart through your eyes and ears. What goes into your eyes and ears will get into your heart and come out of your mouth.

(Brood of vipers! How can you being evil, speak good things? For out of the abundance of the heart the mouth speaks). (Matt. 12:34)

What comes out of your mouth is what will be manifested in your life. Every word you speak is painted on the canvas of your life, sooner or later you're going to have a complete picture. "Watch your mouth, what you say is what you get". If you keep speaking sickness, death, and lack, this is all you're going to get, but, if you will speak the word of God, life, health, and prosperity, that's what you will have.

Faith comes by hearing and hearing by the word of God. Without the word in your hearing, you will have no faith in your heart, one of the requirements for applying the word to your life is having faith, or, "not doubting in your heart", if you are going to see God's word manifested in your life, you must begin to say what the word say. You must speak the word over your circumstances until your circumstances conform to the word. Believe it or not, your situations, your circumstances, your mountains have ears, if they didn't have ears, Jesus would not have said, "You can say to this mountain" (Mark 11:23). That mountain of sickness, that mountain of lack, poverty, stress, depression, oppression, whatever your mountain may be, if you will deposit the word in your heart until it becomes life, and open your mouth and speak the word of God to your mountain, it must obey your faith. This is what I did when my husband was stricken with a crippling stroke. When I began to search for the answer to, how do I apply the word? I did not realize that my first test would be with someone close to me, (my husband), nor did I realize that it would be a test of this magnitude.

My husband (James), has preached the healing message of Jesus Christ to thousands of people, thousands have been healed, saved and delivered from every imaginable thing. In 1987 he became the pastor of a good sized congregation; there he continued to preach the same message.

April 19, 1993 was a morning like any other morning, my husband got out of bed and got dressed for work, my son left for school, I proceeded to clean the house, just another normal, routine, run of the mill day. When I got to the kitchen to do the dishes, I was standing at the sink, when I suddenly felt a strange dark feeling come over me. I thought about my children, but it didn't seem to be coming from them. I begun to pray, but the feeling grew stronger, until it seemed like I could see my husband, and he appeared to be lost or confused somehow. At that time he was in law enforcement working for the county's Sheriff's department. I called the department and asked to speak to him, they tried to reach him on the radio, but received no answer, the dispatcher said, "Mrs. Brown, we can't find him anywhere" I said, "please find him because something is wrong". Meanwhile James had stumbled out of the car into a local store, he was confused, his speech was slurred, and he couldn't remember any phone numbers. The owner of the store knew him, so she quickly realized that something was wrong, she called the Sheriff's department, when the dispatcher called me back, he said, "Mrs. Brown, we've located him, but we are taking him to the doctor's office", ok, I will meet you there. When the dispatcher hung up, the first words out of my mouth was, "not today, Mr. devil, there will be no dieing at my house today, he may die another time, another day, but not today!". I raced to the doctor's office, breaking every speed law in the book and then some. When I got to the doctor's office, they were getting ready to send him to the hospital. When we arrived at the hospital, they took him in right away, the doctors and nurses were very kind. After they took him in the back, the first thing I did was pick up a bible and begun to speak the word over his life. After he had on a white hospital gown for a while, the gown started turning yellow, I did not know what to make of this, I called the nurse, she took one look at him, her eyes popped, she ran out of the room to get the doctor, she said, "his blood pressure has gone through the roof", meanwhile his arm and leg was being drawn more.

We Were Healed

The diagnosis is evident, the prognosis is grim. The doctor says, the length of his hospital stay will be no less than six months, if or when he leaves the hospital, he can look forward to a wheelchair for the rest of his life, and the crazy thing is, my husband seem to be willing to accept this, but not me. I have not been filling my heart with the word of God and setting a watch over my mouth, just to accept this report. I will believe the report of the Lord, "by whose stripes we were healed." You don't have to accept anything less than what the word of God says, just because the devil say die, you don't have to stop breathing. I remember thinking, "with the stripes of Jesus, we were healed", that's what the word says and that's what I am going to say. I put my hand on him and prayed, declaring, "with the stripe that wounded Jesus you are healed", I begun reading every scripture that I could find pertaining to healing. The doctors and nurses did their job, but I knew that, that just wasn't enough. I knew that I had a job to do, but I wanted my familiar tools, my bible, my anointing oil, tape player, and some word tapes, so I called my daughter to bring them to me.

For many hours that night I spoke the word of God, I prayed every kind of prayer that I knew, I bound every devil that I could think of, I read the scriptures for hours, finally, about three in the morning I was so tired, I just had to get some rest, I crawled into bed beside him. There were times when I would lay on top of him, believing that I could impart health and healing into his body. I cannot explain it, I just knew if I slept close to him, life and health would be transferred to him.

The next morning when I awoke, the first thing I did was check to see if he was still alive, praise God, he's still alive, but the stroke has cause more damage. I was sorry that I looked. Things looked really bad. (hopeless really), but I'm not moved by what I see, I'm moved only by the word of God. I picked up the word and started over again. I read all of the scriptures again, laid my hands on him and prayed again, by the time I got through, the nurse was there to begin her daily routine, meds, check vitals, bath and more tests. When she took him out of the room, I wen across the street for coffee, when I returned, my daughter had arrived with my things.

After about four hours of testing, they brought him back to the room, I read (James 5:13-18), anointed him with oil, prayed the prayer of faith again, concluding with, "with the stripes of Jesus, we were healed" thank God it is done now! Each time I read the scriptures and prayed, I reminded the Lord of,

> (P(IS. 55:11), "So shall my word be that goes forth out of my mouth, it shall not return unto me void. But it shall accomplish what I please, and prosper in the things for which I sent it". And S. 107:20), He sent His word and healed them, and delivered them from their destruction".

He did not look or acted healed, it doesn't seem to be working, but I can't give up now. I must forge ahead, I must press forward toward the mark. I believe with my whole heart that God is able to restore him to complete health and wholeness, so, I will hold on to my confession of faith. When I got tired talking I played Kenneth and Gloria Copeland's tapes on healing.

When I felt rested, I turned the tape player off and started speaking the word again. Things did not look any better, they just seemed to get worse, I had to keep reminding myself, "what you say, is what you get, so watch your mouth," Look not at what you can see, the things you see now are only temporary, they are subject to change in a moment. Look to the things eternal which are not subject to change. (2Corn. 4:13-18). God gave me many comforting scriptures, but things still looked bleak. My mind, my flesh, everything human in me wanted to give up, but my spirit said, "hold on to your confession of faith".

On the fourth night of our stay at the hospital, I had a dream I dreamt that they took my husband to do some exploratory surgery to find out why the stroke was doing so much damage, but they were taking so long to bring him back to the room or come and tell me anything, I went down to the O.R. to find out what was taking so long, when I got there, I saw him laying on a stretcher, dressed in his deputy uniform, he was dead. I could not believe it, I screamed so loud, I woke myself up, it was so horribly real. When I realized that it was a dream, I got up and started praying, binding the spirit of death, loosing the word of life for the next two hours. At one point, my husband got really upset with me, about "all that praying, speaking the word and anointing him with oil" he started yelling at me to "shut up and go home, don't tell me about God, look at me, I'm crippled and my hand is useless, I'm not healed, I'll just take the wheelchair". Then I got angry and started yelling at him, "OH NO YOU WILL NOT, when you go home you will be well and whole, with the stripes of Jesus, you are healed". I made up my mind right then, I am not going home until I take him with me well and whole, I will speak the word until I am blue in the face or until God shows up. This I know, the word of God is not always a quick fix, but it is a sure fix. You just have to be willing to stick wit it, no matter how long it takes. If you make up your mind to stand forever, you may not have to stand for very long.

The next morning was Wednesday, two doctors and a nurse came into the room and proceeded to explain to me that they did not understand why the stroke was progressing and causing so much damage. They want to do some exploratory surgery to try and find the answer. They said, "we want to be honest with you, he has about a 15% chance of coming out of the surgery alive, and about an 80% chance of coming out a total vegetable". My mind flashed back to the dream, right away, I said, "NO SURGERY". The doctors got very upset with me, they said, "if you don't let us do the surgery this man could die or become totally paralyzed", well, surgery didn't seem to be offering much better chances, so what have I got to lose by trusting God? "NO SURGERY". The doctor said, "if you do not allow us to operate you will have to sign a form releasing us and the hospital from any liabilities", I said, "give me the paper, the Holy Ghost got this". While I was signing the paper I sensed the presence of the Holy Ghost, he just eased into the room, I thought to myself, "He's here", His presence become so obvious that I saw tears in the eyes of one of the doctors, the nurse was saying, very softly, "thank you Jesus". The doctors became very restless and made up some excuse to get out of the room in a great hurry, when they left the nurse followed behind them smiling and quietly whispering, "thank you Jesus". The presence of the Lord lingered in the room all day. I did not know what God was doing or when he would do it, but I knew he was up to something BIG!

GOD'S WORD MANIFESTED

For the rest of the day I continued praying, speaking the word, anointing him with oil, and playing tapes. I was creating breeding grounds for a miracle, setting the stage for the King of glory to come in. By nine o'clock that night I was so tired, I had to get some rest, so I crawled into bed beside him and fell asleep. I slept for hours. I woke up around one thirty and begun my routine, prayer, the word, anointing with oil and thanking God that the devil is bound and can no longer operate against us.

When I finished reading the scriptures, I ended with, "with the stripes of Jesus, we were healed, now be healed in the name of Jesus". I sat in a chair across from the bed where I could look at him, I cannot tell you why I did that, I just did. Just as I got settled in the chair, I heard, crack, crack, snap, snap, pop, pop, over and over. What is that sound? Where is it coming from? I didn't see anything that could be making a noise like that.

By that time, my husband was awake looking at me. The presence of God was so strong in the room, but what is that sound? Crack-crack, snap- snap, pop-pop. Suddenly, I realized, it's coming from the bed, what in the name of Jesus is going on here? I was too stunned to move, we were so aware of the presence of God in the room we were afraid to say anything, I'm thinking, "GOD IS HERE", it was only a few minutes, but it seemed like hours, it was as though time stopped, then I noticed his hand, his hand was moving, it was straight and normal. I screamed, "look at your hand". Finally, my husband said, "I believe I can walk", that's all I needed to hear, I said, "yes, you can, in the name of Jesus walk". He eased down off the side of the bed, holding onto the bed for support, taking little baby steps, by the side of the bed while I coaxed him, "walk in the name of Jesus". Unsure of himself, he took one baby step at a time, then a few short steps, a little more, by the time we made it to the door it hit him, "with the stripes of Jesus, we were healed". He shouted, "with the stripes of Jesus, I am healed"! When he said that, he started running, shouting aloud, "with the stripes of Jesus, I am healed, I am healed, I am healed, the Lord has healed me".

Three doors down from our room was a gentlemen that was so sick he did not respond to anything or anyone, he had tubes and needles everywhere, in my spare time I would go and stand in his door and pray quietly, he never gave any signs that he knew I was there. When my husband started running and shouting, "I am healed", the man suddenly jumped out of bed, pulled the tubes and needles out and started running behind him, shouting, "with the stripes of Jesus, I am healed". What a mighty God we serve.

My friend, it doesn't matter what sickness or disease has attacked your body, mind, or any part of your life, God wants you well and whole. God wants to heal you everywhere you hurt, and the power of God is available to heal you right now. By faith, receive the healing that belongs to you. Begin confessing the word of God over your life. (Rev. 12:11) "We overcome him by the blood of the lamb and the word of our testimony". Confess the word over your life every day, be persistent, be consistent, be like the woman with the issue of blood, she kept saying to herself "if I can touch the hem of his garment I will be made whole", (Matthew 8:21 AMP). Persistent faith confessions, produces, successful visible possessions. When the commotion was over, and we were back in the room, the nurse came in and said, "I knew there was something different about you two, you are the only patient we ever had with this condition that never complained, you never asked for anything, not even pain medication, every time I came you were praying or playing word tapes, surely the Lord is real. It wasn't three or six months, it wasn't three or six weeks, in seven days the Lord completely healed and restored my husband to health and wholeness. No matter how hopeless your situation may be, or how helpless you may feel. God will help you while you're going through your valley of despair. God will bear you up in His hand, and when the situation becomes unbearable, God will rescue you.

Two days later, my husband and the other gentleman went home completely healed by the power of God.

> "Surely he has borne our griefs, And carried our sorrows, Yet we esteemed Him stricken, Smitten by God, and afflicted. But He was wounded for our transgressions, He was bruised for our iniquities; The chastisement for our peace was upon Him, And by His stripes we are healed". (IS. 53:4-5). "Who Himself bore our sins in His own body on the tree, that we, having died to sins, might live for righteousness, by whose stripes "We Were Healed". (1 Peter 2:24).

Other faith building materials are available from:
Brown's Outreach Ministries
85 Corner Avenue
Salters, South Carolina 29590
E-Mail: brownsoutreachministries@yahoo.com
Myspace:http://www.myspace.com/eagleeye5 (still under construction)
http://www.vemmabuilder.com/12486716
www.myvemma.com/rebeccabr